Janos

Thank you
for joining us!

Janos

Janos

RECIPES &
TALES FROM

PHOTOGRAPHS BY
Geoffrey Clifford

Janos Wilder

A SOUTHWEST RESTAURANT

TEN SPEED PRESS
Berkeley, California

To my mother, for her passion and great taste

1☉
TEN SPEED PRESS
P.O. Box 7123
Berkeley, California 94707

Cover and text design by Nancy Austin and Rebecca Wilder
Type set by Wilsted & Taylor
Photographs by Geoffrey Clifford

Library of Congress Cataloging-in-Publication Data

Wilder, Janos.
  Janos recipes and tales from a southwest restaurant/ by Janos Wilder.
    p.   cm.
  Includes index.
  ISBN 0-89815-655-6 :
    1. Cookery, American—Southwestern style.   2. Cookery, French.
I. Title.
TX715.2.S69W55   1989
641.5979—dc20   89-34132
                                                                      CIP

First printing, 1989

ACKNOWLEDGMENTS

THIS BOOK originated on a hot summer night in 1986 when publisher Phil Wood, in Tucson on business, happened upon the restaurant and began his dinner with three Lobster and Brie Chiles Rellenos. He loved the food, and he sensed that there was a story to be told in the restaurant's thick adobe walls. I am thankful he gave me the opportunity to tell it.

The story would be incomplete without mention of the family, friends, and staff who have supported me in this adventure. My parents, Dave and Joyce, have been there for me at every step, encouraging my education in the many forms it has taken. Rebecca's parents, Harvey and Laurie Bracker, helped us get the business going and have been supportive throughout. Scores of others have contributed to its success.

When I was sixteen, Henry and Violet Hendrickson gave me a chance to cook in their Pizza Parlor in Menlo Park, California. Years later Joe Boches, in Boulder, Colorado, demonstrated that creativity and intelligence could be as much a part of a chef's repertoire as hollandaise and Mornay sauce. At the Gold Hill Inn, Barbara Finn taught me that anything is possible. Later, during a stay in France at the invitation of Roland Flouren, proprietor of La Réserve restaurant in Bordeaux, Didier Petreau and Pierre Bugat showed me how to put everything together with deliciously inspired cooking.

David Tiers, our good friend and attorney, advised me during the seemingly endless procession of meetings and negotiations that were needed to establish the restaurant. Rory McCarthy gave vision to our dream and worked tirelessly to bring it to life. Andy Maas, then director of the Tucson Museum of Art, helped steer us through the maze of committees that came to support our venture. Andy is responsible for our being in our historic location.

Janos wouldn't be nearly the restaurant it's become without its managers, Ellen Burke Van Slyke, Elizabeth Woolls, and now, Andy Haratyk, each of whom took my vision for the restaurant and made it their own. They in turn have been supported by a succession of talented and loyal people, a staff that regardless of the individuals on it at any particular time has always felt like family to me.

In putting this book together I have had the unquestioning support and patience of George Young and Phil Wood at Ten Speed Press; their one rule was that I "enjoy the process!" Geoffrey Clifford is responsible for the stunning photography. His easygoing nature, technical brilliance, and keen eye helped make a potentially stressful task fun and exciting. Ron McBain, from the Plantsman, donated the flowers that helped beautify the interior shots. In the restaurant, my sous-chef, Neal Swidler, took charge of the kitchen and with an excellent and eager crew continued to prepare extraordinary meals while I was busy with the book. Neal's enthusiasm and passion are also evident in the food photographs, where his steady hand and sense of composition helped create the pictures in this book. Cass Johnson, my office manager, had to hang her "miracle flag" on more than one occasion in order to put my handwritten manuscripts onto the computer before the early afternoon Federal Express pickup. On the receiving end of the overnight deliveries was my editor, Carol Henderson. Carol's patience, unfailing good nature, technical mastery, and attention to detail have made sense of these garbled words.

Any credit I've received personally must be given equally to my wife, Rebecca. She has stood alongside me throughout and shared in every tough decision we've had to make. Her help, guidance, good sense, and insistence on excellence are largely responsible for creating and sustaining the restaurant and for the scope and look of this book. Through all of this, she has created a home for us and raised our son, Ben, who is now twice as old as when I first met Phil Wood.

Lastly I want to thank our many friends in the town of Gold Hill, Colorado, who nurtured Rebecca's and my young relationship and encouraged my professional aspirations. I wrote much of this book during the last two summers while cradled there in the bosom of the Rockies.

CONTENTS

CONTINUED ➙

Opening Night

THE FIRST TIME I served lobster and papaya with champagne sauce to a customer was on opening night, an occasion full of tension and excitement. The restaurant was enchanting, with low lights and the flicker of table candles casting a warm glow against peach-colored adobe walls. As our first guests arrived, the sounds of conversation began filling the rooms. Ellen, the restaurant's manager and *maîtresse d'hôtel*, and Rebecca, my wife, greeted the guests. The waiters, confident after a week of rehearsals, were elegant and eager to serve. I was at my place on the cooking line, surrounded by the ingredients and utensils needed for the evening's meals and anxiously awaiting the first orders.

Those last moments seemed to drag on as I checked and rechecked the temperature of the grill and made numerous nervous visits to the front of the house. When the first order finally made its way to the kitchen, my assistant Suzanne and I began the steps of a dance that we would repeat throughout the evening. The first appetizers ordered were snails in puff pastry and Mussels Castroville. Both went out beautifully. Tender, plump snails nestled in puff pastry were presented in a reduced garlic sauce that was shiny from its finishing of pecan butter and colorful with a confetti of finely chopped tomato. In Mussels Castroville, mussels, freshly steamed and removed from their shells, rested on a bed of finely diced prosciutto and tomato which was itself cradled in an artichoke bottom coated with a luxurious mousseline sauce and gratinéed to give it a crisp, dappled skin. As these appetizers left the kitchen, more orders came in. Smoked salmon was composed with a cream dill sauce and capers; filo dough stuffed with pesto and goat cheese was baked to order.

The night began to flow, roughly at first, but with an underlying rhythm. We prepared and delivered salads, and I began to cook the various main courses. While medallions of beef tenderloin grilled, their sauce of rich veal stock, brandy, port, and truffles reduced on the burner. Sweetbreads were flamed in sauternes and simmered with shallots, cream, and fresh herbs, then sprinkled with pistachios and served with bordelaise braised onions. Suzanne blanched and cooked vegetables to complete the composed dinner plates. Opening night vegetables were snow peas, baby carrots, chayote squash, and zucchini—all perfectly trimmed and meticulously arranged with the main courses.

We were in the thick of it, all burners on and sauté pans flashing, when the first order for lobster came in. I had been waiting for this. It was a dish I had thought up in France a year and a half earlier and had fleshed out on my return to Tucson. I saw it as a metaphor for my entire cooking philosophy—a spectacular dish that combined the fundamentals of nouvelle cuisine with the ingredients of the American Southwest. The dish calls for lobster tail meat removed from its shell and sliced, quickly simmered in champagne with a fine julienne of carrot and a drizzle of mesquite honey, and reduced with cream. The lobster and its sauce are arranged around a layered carrot and spinach mousse and garnished with slices of papaya.

As I called the order down to Suzanne for her to heat the mousse, the first reviews were coming back from the dining rooms. We were a hit! By this point we were all floating, our tension gone and in its place pride and excitement. I put the final touch on the lobster, a simple sprig of spearmint to unite the dish with a burst of color, flavor, and freshness. I paused to watch as the waiter placed the dish on his tray. Moments later Rebecca came back to deliver the news. The customer had never seen anything like it before, and for that matter never wanted to again. "How dare I take a lobster tail out of its shell and ruin it with cream and papaya and such frivolity? What were those silly little vegetables and where was the drawn butter and baked potato?" He wanted to know what kind of restaurant we were running! Ellen soon came back to join Rebecca and me in a quick conference. While I was disappointed by my guest's reaction to a dish I had cooked perfectly, it was clear that our first responsibility was to try to satisfy him. The lobster had been prepared properly, as designed, and the dish perfectly executed. We apologized for the gentleman's displeasure and did not charge for the dish. He refused to make another selection and left dissatisfied.

I knew we had lost a customer that night, but something more significant had occurred. In the lobster dish, we had created a concept that was entirely new to the Southwest. We would be tested repeatedly in the months to come, but we were confident. The building was beautiful, the service personal and intelligent, and the food delicious and exciting. The incident with the lobster has never been repeated. That first night was an auspicious beginning for our venture, which to this day remains an experiment in creativity, cooperation, and faith.

A Trip to the Market
in Bordeaux

In 1982 I spent a few months in Bordeaux thanks to Roland Flouren, owner of the restaurant La Réserve. We had met half a year earlier in Santa Fe, and over dinner I persuaded Roland to let me come and learn from his staff. At La Réserve I met Pierre Bugat and Didier Petreau, who were to have a great influence in helping me develop my own culinary style.

Pierre used to take me to market with him. We would leave early in the morning and, winding our way through the dark narrow streets of Pessac into downtown Bordeaux, would arrive just as dawn slowly uncovered the bustle of the marketplace, with vendors readying their stalls for the morning's business. First stop was always the café for espresso and croissants. Here Pierre would renew friendships built over years of making these expeditions. A short gregarious man in his mid-thirties, Pierre had been chef at La Réserve for many years. He learned his craft from Roland's father, the original patron of La Réserve. As a boy, Pierre worked his way up through the kitchen at La Réserve and then moved on to the famous Troigros and Haeberlin kitchens. When he returned to La Réserve it was to take over as chef. During my stay, he was serving as kitchen manager, having temporarily stepped aside as working chef to allow Didier Petreau creative license in the kitchen. Didier was a young man of twenty-four, a rising star among French chefs, full of love for his work. Roland Flouren had brought him in to update the menus with the innovations of nouvelle cuisine. Didier and

Pierre worked well together, while Pierre kept the kitchen organized and stocked, supervising the apprentices supporting the young chef, Didier worked on the cooking line creating magnificent light dishes of beauty and substance.

In the café, Pierre talked to his friends, the vendors, growers, and other chefs in for their day's shopping. After comparing notes, it was off through the stalls of the marketplace. Bordeaux's commercial market is a large, permanently tented square open to the air on all sides and surrounded by small shops selling veal, pork, beef, lamb, bread, cheese, cream, and a myriad of other supplies. As we went along, Pierre stopped at friends' stalls. Always in a joyous, friendly mood he exchanged hugs, kisses, and greetings as he inspected the day's produce. We set aside white asparagus with crisp stalks and tips just turning to purple; slender, young *haricots verts* (string beans), early-season wild strawberries; and baby carrots with tufts of green spilling over the side of the farmer's basket. Lettuces of all types were brought out for our examination. Pierre chose lime-green butter lettuces, bitter arugula, delicate mâche, and tight purple heads of radicchio.

From the produce section we walked to the permanently tiled and plumbed stalls where fish was sold. Here we found oysters and mussels fresh from their beds in the bay at Arcachon, crayfish a delicate pink and longer than their Louisiana cousins, and all varieties of bass, turbot, sole, trout, and John Dory. We shucked a sea scallop to inspect its ring of bright orange roe. The fishmongers packed up our choices as we went off to buy veal, meat, and dairy products.

The French have the same respect for freshness in their poultry as in their fish and produce. Chickens fresh and plump are brought to market with feathers plucked to the neck and with head, feet, and innards still attached. At the *boucherie* where roasts are meticulously tied and displayed, we bought racks of veal and whole carcasses of spring lamb. Next, to the *fromagerie* to choose from scores of different shapes and styles of goat cheese, then to the dairy for cream so thick that it could be brought to a froth with just a couple of flicks of a long balloon flex whip.

As we made our way back through the marketplace to collect the goods that had been set aside for us, an older woman beckoned to Pierre from a stall we had passed by earlier to avoid the crowds. She greeted him with a kiss on both cheeks and a warm hug. I watched as she reached her weathered and calloused hands below her display table and brought out a plain bag. Motioning Pierre closer, she pulled out a treasure—the season's first tarragon, which, about two ounces in all, she had reserved for her friend Pierre. To me, this exchange was the soul of French cooking—an intimate and loving relationship with food and between the people who grow it and those who prepare it.

Didier greeted us when we returned to La Réserve, his eyes flashing with excitement in anticipation of the products we had brought with us. As the truck was unloaded, he inspected each item while carrying on an animated conversation with Pierre about the day's menu. The lettuces would be tossed in a light dressing of lime, garlic, and walnut oil with blanched *haricots verts* and a slice of terrine of foie gras, then garnished with thin slices of dry cured duck breast. The white asparagus would be peeled, blanched, and composed using a rectangle of puff pastry set on a pool of chive beurre blanc sauce offset with a slice of black truffle. Didier would teach the apprentices how to break down the lamb and prepare it in three ways: the leg boned, but left intact to be stuffed with garlic and fresh herbs and then roasted; the loin cut into rib chops for grilling; and the chuck and trim braised with baby spring vegetables in individual casseroles.

Cooks and apprentices began setting up their stations, preparing stocks on the stove, trimming vegetables, fish, and meats, and attending to numerous details for lunch service. Didier and Pierre made their final menu decisions. Oysters fresh and briny would be served simply, on the half shell with lemon. Sea bass would be cut into thin, translucent slices, layered raw on a buttered serving plate and brushed with a mix of blanched orange zest, orange juice, and butter; it would then be flash-broiled under the salamander at the last moment to caramelize the sugar from the orange with the raw butter. The precious tarragon made its appearance in a sauce of fish fumet reduced with a bouquet garni, some tarragon, white wine, shallot, and a little garlic. This preliminary sauce was strained, then slightly reduced with cream, the remaining tarragon being introduced at the last moment so that each taste would be alive. The sauce was used to nap the sea scallops which were sautéed with their bright orange roe attached and peeking through the green and white sauce.

Here was the essence of French nouvelle cuisine—extraordinary raw ingredients lovingly hand selected and prepared to order. Menus were written twice daily to take advantage of fresh and seasonal products. Each dish was well thought out and meticulously composed with an eye toward flavor, color, shape, and texture. The recipes Didier created were, for the most part, straightforward, and they were always designed for vitality, lightness, and flavor. Each ingredient was selected for its freshness and flavor and each flavor was meant to be tasted as a discrete sensation.

The rules of nouvelle cuisine are flexible, relying on the creative interpretation of the chef to get the most from the ingredients. Although the teachings of Escoffier, Carême, and other masters from the past have not been discarded, they are no longer considered an end but rather a point of departure. Nouvelle cuisine is a process of experimentation and discovery, of constantly working with ingredients in innovative and creative ways. The chef, freed from the dogma of ritualistic classical cooking, can assess ingredients and combine them in ways that will allow them to best assert their flavor.

But with freedom a chef must also assume responsibility. Creative license is earned only after years of training and practice; and once earned, it must be taken seriously, not as whimsy or flight of fancy. A chef must be well skilled in all forms of cooking techniques in order to have the flexibility to use ingredients properly. He or she must have an acute sense of taste and an intuitive feel for combining flavors. But most of all, a chef must have respect, not only for the ingredients and craft but for clients as well. In a restaurant a chef creates not only for self-satisfaction but also for the pleasure of the guests. Innovation, creativity, and inspiration become trivial if not exercised in the pursuit of pleasing the client. This is a delicate balancing act, involving educating clients on the one hand and staying in touch with their needs and desires on the other. The infamous abuses of nouvelle cuisine have usually occurred in two ways: In the first, the chef has not developed sufficient skill and understanding of the medium to combine ingredients effectively and to execute proper cooking techniques. In the second instance, the skilled but arrogant chef loses touch with the clientele and creates only for his or her own ego. In both cases, the marketplace proves a sure and efficient remedy to correct the imbalance.

For me, the atmosphere created by the inspired and respectful French nouvelle cuisine was the impetus for developing my own cooking style. I wanted to use the principles I had learned from Pierre and Didier and apply them to the ingredients of the American Southwest. I did not want to become a "southwestern" chef, but an American chef using regional ingredients with nouvelle techniques and sensibilities. My part of the country is a treasure land of wonderful ingredients—with all varieties of peppers from sweet to hot, herbs, tart nopale cactus pods, the sweet syrup of the prickly pear. Papayas and mangos come from Mexico, wonderful fresh cabrilla, a sea bass, is caught in the waters of Baja California. My dream was to integrate Ttese and other ingredients into a complete cuisine that emphasized the foods and lifestyles of my region while drawing upon the bounty of the entire American harvest.

Hiring, Building, Rehearsing— Getting Ready to Open

ELLEN BURKE VAN SLYKE came into our lives amid clouds of construction dust and the cacophony of jackhammers. I had set up temporary offices in one of the interior dining rooms to be as far as possible from the construction crew, which was digging trenches for electrical, gas, and water lines. Still, the noise and grime were inescapable. Lining my office were numerous dining room tables recently purchased at auction, on which were scattered the scores of china, glasses, and silverware samples we were considering. My desk was a table set against one wall, equipped with a telephone and buried under piles of papers and drawings. It was mid-September, 105 degrees outside and hotter inside as the adobe walls radiated heat inward.

I had placed an ad in the local papers to test the waters for available waiters, cooks, and managers. Although I was comfortable with my own knowledge of the back of the house and delighted with the team of Rory (our interior designer and friend) and Rebecca working on the interiors, none of us knew much about organizing the service staff and managing the front of the house—in other words, taking care of our guests. We were well aware of our inexperience but had no clear plan for filling the void. Then Ellen responded to the ad.

She impressed me immediately with her air of competence and self-assurance. She was dressed crisply and professionally but with a hint of the flamboyance that I would come to know as her trademark. Although the ad had been for waiters, her resumé reflected extensive experience managing and waiting in highly regarded restaurants in Seattle and Boston.

Ellen and I talked for three hours in the sweltering heat and noise that afternoon. As she explained her philosophy of fine dining and described how to provide graceful service, it became clear that she was extraordinarily knowledgeable. I learned her techniques for how to empty ashtrays, unfurl napkins with flair but not ostentation, serve drinks, present food, present and pour wine, divide entrées, handle requests and complaints, answer the phone, and juggle reservations. Ellen's view of waiting gave life to a spirit of hospitable, gracious service that was correct without being stuffy or pretentious. In short, she could supply the missing link—how to run the front of the house.

Just as I had seen in her someone to carry out my dreams, Ellen saw in the restaurant the opportunity to run her own show. After years of answering to employers, she would now have the autonomy to set up the front of the house, the wine list, the bar, and the service staff as she saw fit. More than being a manager, Ellen would be *maîtresse d'hôtel* in what would quickly become the finest restaurant in town. While I was totally consumed with the kitchen during our first few months in operation, Ellen's personality and charm personified the image that people had of Janos. Many customers may never have met me, but everyone knew Ellen. It was Ellen, as much as Rebecca, Rory, or I, who created Janos.

The last couple of months before opening were hectic and full of decision making as Ellen elaborated the details of service and style and wrote an exhaustive training manual. Our goal was to have employees who were not only competent but who could serve as ambassadors for the restaurant as well. Because of the uniqueness of our building and concept, the entire staff had to be prepared to answer a myriad of questions ranging from the age of the building and the ancestry of its original owners to queries about adobe building techniques to descriptions of ingredients in menu items. All of this information is contained in the manual, which is updated as needed to include new artists, policy changes, etc.

My opening crew and those hired in the first few months developed into a great team. They embraced the restaurant and Ellen's standards for precision and excellence while settling into their roles and accommodating the wishes of the rush of new customers. Among my first waiters was Elizabeth Woolls. Liz, a young Englishwoman with lilting London accent, quickly became our star waiter and soon assumed headwaiter responsibilities. Later she became assistant manager. When Ellen moved on after a year and a half, Liz took on full management responsibilities. She gracefully and confidently guided us through a smooth transition, asserting her own style while building on a strong tradition of excellent, refined service. Like Ellen, she has all the qualities of intelligence, quick and independent thinking, thoroughness, honesty, and loyalty that I look for in a manager.

Finding an opening kitchen staff presented its own set of problems. The cuisine we were creating required knowledgeable, skilled personnel and at that time, Tucson did not have a reserve of professional cooks from which to choose. I knew I would have trouble hiring a trained staff but felt we could get by with a strong sous-chef and competent baker while I trained the remaining kitchen staff. I went about hiring in a thorough manner, quizzing applicants about their knowledge, checking references, and trying to get a feel for how the individuals would function under pressure. The sous-chef I chose had opened other local restaurants and came highly recommended for both his reliability and skill. My pastry chef had good training, and my pantry cooks were eager.

After weeks of delays, snags, setbacks, and late deliveries, the physical restaurant was in place. The dining rooms, bar, and public rooms looked stunning. Rebecca and Rory were making final decisions on art to be hung, and Ellen was finishing up hiring and writing schedules. I was in the kitchen with equipment installers calibrating ovens, checking out the steamer, and adjusting refrigeration. After months of planning and agonizing over the details of equipment purchases and placement, my kitchen was about to come to life. On the following day the kitchen staff was scheduled to come for preliminary training and prep work. I had previously issued them the recipes they would be using so that they would be prepared to work. I myself couldn't have been more excited and eager to cook. And then the phone rang. It was my sous-chef calling to say he'd broken his arm and was off to southern Florida to recuperate and wouldn't be returning.

I was devastated, my enthusiasm dashed. One of my key people was gone, and I didn't have time to find an experienced replacement. Up to this point I had taken one step at a time, keeping an eye on the whole picture and moving toward completion in a logical sequence. I had treated previous obstacles as challenges to be met and conquered. But now I felt the enormity of the entire project weighing on me and for the first time I was overcome with doubts. I knew I couldn't do without a sous-chef and began questioning the wisdom of starting a business too large to accomplish by myself.

Even in this moment, though, I knew there was someone I could turn to. Dora Bursey, Rebecca's best friend from high school, was on the patio doing some decorative planting for our outside dining area. Dora is one of the most remarkable people I know, having accomplished more in her thirty-two years than most people do in their entire lives. In school she studied English literature, fine arts, and nuclear physics while receiving a degree in education. She is an accomplished artist, has run her own building contracting business, and, with her father, has operated the local Cadillac dealership. These accomplishments notwithstanding, one of Dora's best talents is cooking. In my personal list of the top ten meals ever, two have been made by Dora.

After a while I composed myself and walked to the patio to discuss the situation with Dora. I was nervous about asking her to take over the position and fumbled while outlining the circumstances. It was one thing to ask a friend to help with planting, quite another to invite her to be my sous-chef, a fifty-hour-a-week job for which she had no formal training. Dora let me off the hook by suggesting the obvious, and traded in her gardening clothes for cook's checked pants.

Asking a great home cook to work in a restaurant is a little like asking a home gardener to become a farmer. The transition from hobby to vocation exposes the rigors of the profession as the glamor is replaced by grueling hours and the pressure of production. If work in a professional kitchen is ever glamorous (which I doubt), it was certainly not so during those first few weeks. Yet Dora rose to the challenge superbly, even helping to establish some of the systems still in effect today.

In preparation for the opening, we had scheduled a week of trial lunches for friends and associates who would act as our guinea pigs. Three days before the lunches were to begin, I called in the kitchen staff. We now had eight days to mold a relatively inexperienced crew into a coordinated, skilled team producing great food. It was a challenge everyone rose to with enthusiasm. The first day we learned the layout of the kitchen and set up systems for the walk-in refrigerator, storage, and receiving. Everything was given a home and everyone learned where it was (although I still have trouble finding a potato peeler). As the first deliveries arrived, raw products were put up. When that first afternoon ended, we had a clean, organized kitchen. By noon the next day the first batch of bread had come out of the ovens. That afternoon we tested recipes for salad dressings, working them until we got the results I wanted. Suzanne practiced *tourné* work (carving vegetables into regular shapes) and cold sauces. Dora and I had time for little more than to go from person to person offering guidance. The third day we concentrated on the menus, and by that afternoon we had prepared every item on the lunch menu as well as some garnishes and presentations for dinner. Every step was a new experience as the staff learned how to make food they had never seen before on equipment they had never used. Our first successes were exhilarating; while learning our individual roles we were also beginning to coalesce into a team.

On the morning of that third day I could see progress all around me and was confident we would be ready on time. Workmen and painters were putting the final touches on the building, Rebecca and Rory were hanging pictures. My prep schedule for the morning included grinding beef and I thought what fun it would be to serve lunch for everyone. Although we weren't scheduled to bake any bread and the refrigerator had no produce other than spinach, I thought everyone would be happy to share a simple meal, hamburger steak and sautéed spinach.

I put out the word that we were cooking lunch to be served at 12:30. As I walked through the dining room back into the kitchen, the anticipation was palpable. Even the workmen were eager, and Rory was particularly excited to see what I would produce. I immediately knew my offer had been premature. These people were far too excited for what they were going to get. After months of hearing about the cuisine, they were anxious to try it and were expecting the full treatment at a lunch I was treating as a lark. I tried to explain my intentions to dampen the enthusiasm, but the lunch had taken on a life of its own.

Things got worse. Dora and I broke down an inside round of beef and began to feed it through the grinder attachment to the mixer that I had bought used at an auction. Only when the meat backed up and slowly squirted through the grinder did we discover that our cutting blades were as dull as stones. Lunch was half an hour away. We tried to salvage the meat by grinding at various speeds using every cutting blade and die we had. Nothing worked. The more we fiddled, the tougher and grainier the meat became.

When I had first announced lunch there were eight of us, by noon there were twelve. Dora and I did our best to form the meat into patties and put them on the grill to cook. I sautéed the spinach in some butter with garlic, salt, pepper, and balsamic vinegar and stretched the small amount we had to cover twelve orders. We had no sodas or beer to offer, just tepid water, and not even any catsup with which to disguise the hamburger.

The crew assembled and sat around the table that Rebecca set with linen in one of the dining rooms. No one seemed to mind the lack of beverage, since the food would be the focus and everyone was hungry. Conversation was animated all about the trial-run lunches that were to begin on Monday. Dora, the cooks, and I prepared the plates, each with one tough, grainy hamburger and a dollop of spinach. Conversation stopped as we delivered the food, and nothing was said as people took their first bites. I felt my face get redder and redder as the silence continued. Finally one of the painters said politely, "Boy, this is great! Thanks for lunch."

The tension was broken when Rebecca burst out laughing. I explained the situation and gave my apologies, which everyone seemed to accept good-naturedly. I was humbled and relieved to have this misstep behind me—until I glanced at Rory. His face was sober with disappointment. A master craftsman and designer, he had worked faithfully for months on a project whose success hinged entirely on my ability to cook. If this meal was any indication, Rory knew we were in serious trouble. There was nothing I could say to calm his fears. His faith was being tested, and he would have to wait a little longer to see what I was really capable of producing.

Compared to that first lunch, the week of trial runs proceeded smoothly. We had invited friends, associates, and people who had worked with us on the project to be our customers for the first week. In return for letting us learn from experience, they got free lunch. Each day we improved, and by Friday we had worked out many of the glitches and were eager to serve the paying public the following Monday.

Word about the restaurant was already spreading. Local papers had run features on us in the business section and on the last Friday of our trial-lunch week, the local NBC affiliate did a spot on us for the evening news.

Our marketing strategy was to start slowly, relying on word of mouth. We did no opening advertising because we wanted to let the business grow gradually as we perfected our execution. Worse than too little business at first would be more business than we could handle well. From a number of mailing lists for lawyers, doctors, country clubs, and cultural groups, we had targeted about five thousand people who we felt were our potential customers. Rebecca designed an elegant opening announcement and mailed it during the week of trial runs. Reservations began to come in almost immediately.

That last Friday before opening, we held a kind of family dinner. We invited Rebecca's immediate family, uncles, and first cousins, and my family came from California. In addition to relatives we invited our extended family of close friends from Tucson and even had a surprise visit from one of our best friends in Gold Hill, Colorado.

This would be the real debut for me—my first chance to cook the dinner menu. It was also our only chance to practice our dinner routine. The excitement and tension produced by a successful week of lunch rehearsals was mounting. Rebecca brought in a TV so we could watch the news spot shot that afternoon. It was thrilling to see ourselves on TV, to see customers' reactions, and the coverage helped to validate our efforts. The entire staff was in great spirits as we got ready to serve dinner. We had asked our guests to call and make reservations from 7:00 to 8:30 so that the distribution would be even throughout the evening. We certainly didn't want a frenzied first night in the kitchen.

By 6:30 we were ready and eager. By 7:00 we were nervous again. Rebecca and Ellen were at the front door to receive our guests. By 7:30 no one had arrived, and we knew we had a family conspiracy on our hands. Everyone wanted to come at the same time to make a party of it. By 8:00 we had prepared only a few appetizers when the tickets started coming in one after the other. Everyone was eating at about the same time.

I wasn't quite prepared for this rush, but we equipped ourselves well. The system I had devised was working. Suzanne and I moved well together. It was my first night cooking dinner professionally in over two years, and I was a little rusty but soon fell into the routine. I was pleased with the results, and although the system needed refining, I was delighted with our overall performance.

When I went into the dining room after cleaning up the kitchen, the party was in full swing. I got some helpful criticism, but on the whole, everyone was satisfied and in a mood to celebrate. We were also having a reunion that night. The last time this group had been together was at our wedding three years earlier in Colorado. Rebecca and I slipped out of work mode and joined the party. It was a joyous evening for us, and we went to sleep that night proud of a successful week of trial runs. But I think the most relieved person that evening must have been Rory; he found out I really did know how to cook.

The next evening we were expecting a turnout of 250 to 300 for our pre-opening cocktail party. This time I would not be in the kitchen during service. I had rented a tuxedo for the occasion and was going to join Rebecca and Ellen in meeting guests and showing off the restaurant.

Almost everyone invited to the party would be seeing the restaurant for the first time, and I wanted it to be a memorable experience. By the time the cooks arrived at 10:00 a.m. their prep lists were ready, and they went about their tasks. We were preparing about thirty different hot and cold appetizers to be passed. Earlier in the week we had dry-cured salmon for gravlax, smoked turkey breast, made pâtés and terrines, pickled peppers, prepared relishes, and mixed various spreads for canapés. Two bushels of oysters, shucked, were to be served broiled on the half shell with mesquite-smoked bacon, Parmesan, and chilies or topped with red pepper pesto. Twenty pounds of large Mexican shrimp had to be cleaned, then half of them skewed with chayote squash for grilling, the other half poached, chilled, wrapped in roasted Anaheim chilies, and placed on puff pastry with papaya and pomegranate relish.

In the afternoon Ellen and her staff of waiters and bartenders arrived to reset the dining rooms for the party. We intentionally overstaffed for the night so that no one would have to wait for food or drink. I also wanted our guests to meet all of our staff to get to know the quality of people who would serve them when they came to dine.

I left late in the afternoon to pick up my tuxedo and returned with Rebecca shortly before our first guests were expected. Entering the restaurant through the front door, we were immediately enchanted by the warmth and grace of the building. The ambience was comfortable and inviting—the way it must have felt years ago to enter a grand home in an era of gracious hospitality and charm. Our sense of well-being and propriety soothed away the tensions of the previous months of work and worry, as did the warm glow of low lights reflecting the peach of the walls. Soon enough the house would be filled with conversation and bustle, but for those few moments Rebecca and I sat in the lounge and reflected on the accomplishments of the past year.

Our reverie was interrupted when Ellen reminded us that our guests were due to arrive. In the kitchen, canapés, oysters, shrimp, and assorted preparations awaited, all meticulously arranged on silver platters. It was time to call the servers together for a last pep talk before service. This meeting, known as "pre-meal," is our opportunity to go over notes and check in with our staff before service. I described the hors d'oeuvres we would be offering, and stressed the importance of the evening for introducing the restaurant to Tucson. Ellen went over final service pointers. The waiters, eager to serve the public after the week of training and dry runs, seemed confident and poised. I knew we were heading for a splashy and successful opening.

Indeed it was a wonderful night, rather like a sneak preview in its exuberance. The restaurant filled quickly as people walked from room to room visiting with us and each other, admiring the art and architecture, and sampling the food. Our guests felt special and took a real interest in what we were trying to accomplish. Many had been hoping that this sort of establishment would open in Tuscon and were looking forward to trying us for lunch and dinner.

Ellen, Rebecca, and I guided tours and handed out scores of menus. It was a pleasure to meet the people who would become our regular customers and friends of the house. I was especially glad of the opportunity because it would be many more months before I could leave the kitchen and mingle with guests again.

Much of the initial success of the business can be credited to the week of trial runs. We had hired a mature staff with good potential and then given them the chance to learn their jobs at our expense, not at the expense of paying customers. The friends and associates who tolerated our imperfections early in the week forgave us and remained interested in the restaurant. Not only had we achieved our goal of training the crew, we had done so in a way that pulled individuals together into a team that shared the common goals of excelling and making their place of work the very best restaurant they could imagine.

At Home in a Historical Site

JANOS IS IN A VERY special building. As we were searching for a place in which to start the restaurant, our friend Rory McCarthy showed us a block of historical buildings owned by the Tucson Museum of Art. The museum had earlier considered putting a restaurant into one of them—the home of a prominent citizen of Tucson in the 1800s—but nothing had come of it. Yet as we entered Hiram Stevens' house, I sensed immediately that we had found our location: this fine old structure, with its high ceilings and array of simple, intimate spaces, seemed to invite an enterprise that would once again welcome people within its walls and reintroduce a spirit of gracious living. I knew instinctively that our guests would feel comfortable here.

Now, several years later, I like to think that Hiram Stevens would have approved of the business we're running in his home. Mr. Stevens was one of Tucson's first pioneers. Born in Vermont in 1832, he enlisted in the army at age nineteen and was sent to New Mexico to fight the Indians. After his enlistment was up, he moved to southern Arizona in 1856 and lived on a ranch in the Santa Cruz Valley about three miles from where he later built his home.

Tucson in the 1850s was a wild, colorful territory where guns often ruled and the strongest and brightest could make their fortunes. Stevens was rugged and jovial; he was a gambler, a politician, and an astute businessman. His first enterprise in Tucson was supplying army posts with hay and beef. The business thrived, and soon he expanded, bringing in merchandise from San Francisco and selling it to soldiers throughout the territory.

Over the years Stevens flourished. He operated as post trader at Fort

Huachuca near the Mexican border and at Camp Crittenden near Tubac, Arizona. He purchased a ranch in the Sierritas south of Tucson and developed it into one of the finest and most prolific cattle ranches in the region. He also had mining interests in Colorado. Wherever promising commercial activity developed in southern Arizona, Stevens was there, and he was generally successful in getting a piece of the business for himself.

But for all his business acumen and successes, the stories we most delight in telling our guests are about his colorful personality and sense of adventure. The memory of Hiram Stevens is kept alive at Janos as we give nightly tours of the house and retell stories of Hiram's life in the Old West.

One of our favorite stories is of Hiram's courtship of his wife-to-be, Petra Santa Cruz. One day in 1856 Stevens came into town in search of someone to do his laundry. Near the center of town he came to the home of Guadalupe "Lupe" Santa Cruz. Spying the pretty, sixteen-year-old Petra in the back of the house, Stevens instantly decided to marry her. Lupe was shocked. She didn't like Americans and she especially distrusted non-Catholics. She forbade Hiram from having anything to do with her granddaughter; she even refused to do his laundry. But Hiram was known for his perserverance, and he spent the next three years trying to convince the priest who came to Tucson once a year, to baptize him. Finally the priest agreed. Hiram was baptized in 1859 and Lupe, deferring to the wishes of Hiram and Petra, consented to the marriage.

Six years later Stevens built a home for himself and Petra directly across the street from Lupe. The house, which is now the restaurant, was built in Tucson's oldest area. Established in 1776 as a Spanish presidio, the town was originally a fort built to protect the inhabitants of nearby San Xavier Mission. The Stevens' house is thought to have been built on some of the original footings of the presidio wall.

As befitted one of Tucson's leading citizens, Hiram built one of Tucson's grandest homes. It was constructed with four rooms and three fireplaces off of a central corridor, or *zaguán*. Although the architecture was typical of the finest structures of the time, Stevens' home had the highest ceilings and thickest adobe walls in town. Later Stevens enlarged his home by purchasing and incorporating the adjacent house.

In 1979 my landlord, the Tucson Museum of Art, undertook renovation of the Stevens building and restored it to its original magnificence. The ceilings, all at least fourteen feet high, are finished with many of the original saguaro cactus ribs. The adobe walls, some of them over two and a half feet thick, have been repaired, and the building has been modernized with plumbing, electricity, and air conditioning. When we adapted the house to a restaurant in 1983, we did little to change it. Our work was limited to upgrading mechanical features and enclosing the back porch, which once served as Petra's aviary and is now our largest dining room.

The look of the restaurant is largely the inspiration of Rory McCarthy. Rory had made a name for himself by winning national and international competitions in furniture design for his interior design firm in Tucson. Working closely with Rebecca, who developed the color scheme and does all of our graphics, Rory guided our decisions about the interior spaces. The rooms he designed are at once elegant, friendly, historical, and surprisingly contemporary. He left the interior largely untouched except for painting the walls the peachy coral tones that Rebecca chose. For the dining rooms and *zaguan*, he turned to his friends in the local artist community, inviting some to hang their work on our walls. The restaurant now houses a stunning collection of original local art, which seems right at home on the sensuous old walls.

But probably Rory's most conspicuous contribution to the restaurant is the furniture he designed and fabricated. We were all enamored of the magnificent antique pieces we had seen on trips to Nogales—pieces that had been extracted from Mexican haciendas and villas. The feel of the old, worn wood, the massiveness of their construction, and the stark geometry of their lines made them natural choices for our old adobe. Unfortunately, my budget wouldn't allow us to collect antiques. Convinced that this was the kind of furniture we needed, Rory decided to design and construct it himself. He created a bar with painted columns, colored geometric glass, and galvanized metal top, as well as playful bar stools with tripod bases and triangular accents. For the *zaguan*, he fashioned a huge armoire from new and salvaged lumber that he antiqued to look as if it must have once belonged to Hiram. Not only does the armoire hold coats for our guests, but Rory also outfitted it with a secret side panel that opens to reveal the maitre d' stand and telephone. For the lounge Rory built a massive, slightly cracked mirror with an antiqued wooden frame.

To me, the house has much of the same homey, elegant feel that I sense from old photographs of it. According to accounts I've read, Stevens entertained almost as much in the 1860s, '70s, and '80s as we do in his home

Founders of the restaurant:
Ellen Burke Van Slyke, Rebecca Wilder,
and Dora Bursey

The restaurant staff

The zaguan (front hall) of the restaurant

Hiram Stevens' Room

today. Stevens the politician was twice elected to the U.S. Congress as well as to numerous local posts. He frequently entertained government officials and prominent businessmen in his home. One story has him throwing a spontaneous party for two hundred of his supporters during the election campaign of 1874. Years later his daughter Eliza remembered that there were always servants to serve good food and wine. "Everything was always in abundance in the house in which I grew up," she recalled.

Stevens' entrance into national politics during the election for territorial delegate to the U.S. Congress in 1874 provides a glimpse into his character and an insight into how society functioned in Arizona at the time. Stevens had previously served in the state legislature and had been Tucson's first treasurer. In the race for territorial delegate, he ran against R.C. McCormick, an incumbent of several terms who was supported by the territorial and national administrations. Stevens turned to a group of gambling cronies who formed a large and influential network in the territory. Using $25,000 of his campaign funds, Stevens offered to stake them to bets of $1,000, $2,000, or $3,000. If Stevens was elected his friends would keep their winnings; if not, they had nothing to lose. With the gambling community solidly behind him, Stevens' victory was assured, and he was elected by a wide margin.

My staff today tells these and other stories about Hiram Stevens and old Tucson as they escort guests through the various rooms of the house. Sometimes the tours end by the Stevens room, a small dining room we've named for Hiram and Petra. In this room Hiram met with a tragic death by his own hand. Friends relate that in 1893 Hiram was depressed over business reverses. He had also been in poor health for some time. In spite of his deteriorating condition, he joined fellow members of the board of supervisors on a trip to inspect the route of a new road to be built to Nogales. After three or four days of travel, he returned home and, complaining of a severe headache, went to bed. Petra went to rest in another room. Three hours later, Stevens, armed with two revolvers, entered the room where Petra was resting and began speaking to her tenderly. When Petra saw the guns he was carrying, Hiram raised the smaller of the two pistols and shot his wife twice. His first bullet struck her hand and the second glanced off of a silver comb in her hair, which saved her life. Hiram then aimed the large revolver at his own forehead and pulled the trigger, thus ending the life of one of Tucson's most colorful citizens.

Ingredients

WHEN YOUR COOKING RELIES on quality ingredients you have to be certain you can always get the best. So from the very start we organized a network of growers, suppliers, and brokers to provide the products we would require.

Well before I advertised for staff, I placed an ad in the local papers for gardeners. Through my wife's family we are able to get produce directly from brokers in Nogales as Mexican produce enters the U.S. before being distributed throughout the country. Seafood houses in Tucson with connections in Mexico supply us with cabrilla, a firm, white sea bass from the water off Baja California, oysters from the Gulf of Mexico, and sweet shrimp from Guaymas, a port about 200 miles south of us in the Mexican state of Sonora.

The desert and its environs are far from the dry, desolate expanse that many of us picture. Papayas, mangos, chayote squash, and peppers in all colors and flavors grow a short distance from us in Mexico. The desert where we live supplies us with nopales, the tart young pads of the prickly pear cactus, and with prickly pears themselves, the sweet fruit of the cactus. Locally, agricultural research is being conducted to isolate and replant pure strains of native seeds. On occasion we receive gifts, such as native blue corn to grind into flour for baking.

Cultivating sources for the products we use is a never-ending process. Rarely a week passes that I don't learn about a new grower or broker I want to pursue. Sometimes it happens while I'm reading the local paper, which is how I found Brian McNellis.

A biologist by training, Brian raised tilapia in freshwater ponds in the middle of the desert, ninety miles west of Tucson, in Gila Bend. Tilapia is a small, sweet-flavored, mild fish indigenous to the Nile, where it is called St. Peter's fish or Nile perch. It was brought to this country for research purposes because it can reproduce prolifically in crowded conditions and can adapt to either fresh or salt water. Researchers are interested in it as a food source in arid lands, where it can be raised and harvested with relative ease in salt water. Brian recognized that this hardy, good-tasting fish might have commercial value locally and created Gila River Fisheries using a series of abandoned aqueducts in which to raise his tilapia.

As his business began to produce, Brian started selling to local Asian restaurants that prize the fish for its sweet meat and bright silver skin. Soon after I contacted him, he started supplying us also. Now tilapia shows up on my menus in numerous preparations. We generally fillet and grill the fish to bring out the most of its mild flavor and then we garnish it in a variety of ways.

One of my favorite times of the day is when the gardeners deliver. I'll look up from my work station to see a youngster of three or four years clutching in one hand a wicker basket bursting with a rainbow bouquet of Johnny-jump-ups, pansies, portulacas, nasturtiums, and antique roses; the other hand is dragging along mom, who herself is laden with gifts from her garden. Soon my table is overflowing as we sort and weigh tender leaves of arugula, radicchio, mâche, baby romaine, and ruby red lettuce. Bags of miniature radishes with their red shoulders fading into white tips appear alongside a sample of guava flowers, about which mom says casually, "I just threw those in, thought you might like to try them." Indeed! They're sweet and juicy, bursting with flavor from the fruit, and their petite flowers will make an attractive garnish.

Each little package holds its own treasures. The perfume from four different varieties of basil mingles with the aroma of fresh tarragon, just-snipped rosemary, and citrusy lemon thyme. Lugs of tomatoes picked that morning, fifty miles east of us in St. David, are piled on the tables. These are not the perfectly round, uniformly red, hard tomatoes you buy at the grocery store. These tomatoes are slightly irregular in shape and size, bright red, but with skin imperfections—the real McCoy, juicy and full of flavor. I smile as I think of the customer who likes a salad of tomatoes and basil vinaigrette, knowing the pleasure these plump fruit will bring him.

I often think of Pierre and the French markets when I'm surrounded by these treats from my gardeners. I get the same feeling from these people and their harvest that Pierre must get from his friends in Bordeaux. They are part of my extended restaurant family, as important as a waiter or cook. They begin the cycle of food from the ground to the table.

Aside from our locally grown staples, we use a large variety of specialty items—unique goods that are both delicious and unusual and that allow our customers to try foods not readily available to them. We work hard at developing sources that can provide new items to add to the menu. Of course, being unique is not enough by itself; a product must also be of high quality and taste great. It's not my goal to challenge my customers with new things. I want them to be able to try new things I know they will like.

In the spring we bring in morels and fiddlehead ferns from the Northwest or field mushrooms from Italy. I get fresh rabbit and pheasant from California, venison from New Zealand and Texas. A local butcher raises the suckling pigs we use for both special parties and our nightly menus.

Specialty items make up an important part of our menu writing and preparation. Although at the core our cooking relies on the use of local ingredients and southwestern cuisine is certainly our slant, it is a treat for everyone when we have something new to offer. My customers love to experiment, my cooks learn from the exposure and I'm always eager to try new combinations of flavors and textures. Because we write our menus on a daily basis, we can add a new item or dish whenever we find a product that impresses us.

FROM THE SOUTHWEST

The Sonoran desert provides an abundance of foods that are not found elsewhere in the country. These ingredients are the inspiration for much of our cooking. Walking through the desert with my son early on August mornings, we often gather the sweet fruit of the prickly pear cactus to use in the restaurant for sauces or compotes. In spring we pick tender nopale cactus pads for garnish or to cook as a vegetable.

Chili Peppers

To many people chili peppers are synonymous with Mexican food, in everything and always hot. In our cooking, chilies are just one of many ingredients.

Chili peppers are members of the *Capsicum* family, which includes hundreds of different types of chilies. We cook with only a few varieties that are readily available and appropriate to our style.

Chilies get their heat from *capsaicin*, the active ingredient found primarily in the white membrane of the chili, its seeds, and interior. The skin of chilies contains no *capsaicin*, and can be touched with impunity.

Our cooking relies on a delicate interplay and balance of ingredients which allows each flavor to be tasted as a distinct sensation. I avoid the hottest chilies for two reasons: First, they tend to overpower other ingredients in a dish. Second, many of my customers are not used to hot food and would not appreciate the shock of a jalapeño pepper in the mouth or intestinal tract. Anaheims are the chili I use most frequently because they are sweet and mild, with a hint of the heat of their more fiery cousins. But even they are not always predictable. One night I served grilled cabrilla with salsa, Guaymas shrimp, and a lattice of roasted Anaheim chilies. Two days later I received an irate letter from a customer whose wife had suffered the indignity of chili too hot for her system to handle—and on her birthday no less. I had tasted many of the chilies we used that night and found them sweet and mild, exactly what I wanted. But even of the same variety, some chilies are going to be hotter than others.

I learned to roast Anaheim chilies over a barbecue from my wife, Rebecca, who picked up the technique in the marketplace in San Miguel de Allende in Mexico. The chilies are lightly slicked with oil and placed on a grate directly over white-hot coals. As the chilies blacken, they are turned so that the skin is uniformly blistered away from the meat. They are then placed in the folds of a damp cloth to steam the skin cleanly off. When the chilies are cool they are peeled, a slit is cut on their sides, and the seed pod is removed. In this form they are ready for chopping or stuffing for *rellenos*.

In the restaurant we've adopted a different method for peeling Anaheim chilies. We blister them quickly in hot oil, submerge them in ice water to stop the cooking, loosen the skin, and then peel and seed them.

ANAHEIMS   Anaheim chilies are 6 to 7 inches long, 1½ inches wide and shiny green. They are among the mildest chilies and have a slightly sweet flavor with some bite. We use them for stuffing, in salsas, cut into strips and tossed with other peppers as garnish, in salads, and in combination with other chilies when a recipe calls for more heat.

POBLANOS   These dark green, triangular-shaped chilies are 3 to 5 inches long and about 3 inches wide at the stem, tapering to a point. They are more pungent than Anaheims and can be used in all the same ways when a slightly hotter chili is called for.

ANCHOS   Anchos are dried poblanos. They are sweeter than the fresh poblano and can be used in sauces or moles (rich Mexican sauces made from chilies, seeds, nuts, stock, and chocolate). They are often ground for use in commercial chili powder.

PASILLAS   Pasilla chilies are about the same size and shape as anchos but are a chocolate-brown color when fresh. They vary in flavor from mild to hot and are available in Mexican specialty stores in packages labeled mild to hot. We use dried pasillas in our New Mexico Red Chili Sauce.

JALAPEÑOS   Jalapeños are relatively small, 2 inches by 1 inch, and very hot. They should not be used alone because they can overpower other flavors in a dish. To achieve a sweet, full chili flavor without too much heat, we use them in conjunction with the other, milder chilies in some salsas, soups, and stuffings.

CHIPOTLES   Intense and uniquely flavored chipotles are smoke-dried jalapeño peppers. They can add a fiery, smoky taste to stews and sauces, but like the jalapeño, they should be used cautiously.

SERRANOS   Serranos are the hottest chilies we use. They are 1½ to 2 inches long and ¼ to ½ inch wide. They are medium to dark green when young and ripen to a deep red. We dice them very finely and use them as a fiery accent in hearty dishes they will enliven and not dominate. Caution should be used in chopping serranos because their seeds, membranes, and meat can burn your skin. Work with them quickly and wash your hands, utensils, and cutting board immediately after chopping.

Nopales

The young leaves or pads of the prickly pear cactus which grows prolifically in the Sonoran desert are called nopales. They are tart and juicy, similar in texture to okra. Although they have a good flavor for using raw in salads or stews, I prefer them grilled or dipped in egg white and deep-fried. Cooked in this way they lose their sliminess but remain citrusy in flavor and succulent. When you are preparing nopales, wear gloves and carefully remove all stickers and nodules with a sharp paring knife. Rinse the nopales thoroughly after trimming, and be sure to clean your cutting board of all trimmed stickers.

Prickly Pear Fruit

Around my house in August, we harvest the fruit of the prickly pear cactus. These fruits grow after the cactus flowers in the spring. They are mature when they have turned dark red and pluck easily from the cactus leaves. The fruit is protected by small, sharp stickers which we avoid by harvesting with tongs and carefully placing the fruit into thick baskets. At the restaurant we cut the fruit in half lengthwise and carefully scoop out the purplish-red fruit, avoiding the stickers. When the fruit is cooked down and its tiny seeds strained out, it yields a thick, sweet syrup that is wonderful in sauces, compotes, and jellies; it also makes a great margarita.

Chayote Squash

Indigenous to Mexico and Central America, chayote squash is a pale green, pear-shaped vegetable with a thick skin, large seed, and clean cucumber-like flavor. The squash must be peeled, cooked (preferably steamed), and seeded before serving. Its shape is excellent for stuffing, or it can be steamed, cut into quarters lengthwise, sliced like a fan, and cooked on the grill with salt, pepper, garlic, and a brushing of olive oil.

Blue Corn

Blue corn is native to the Southwest, where it has been cultivated for centuries by the Pueblo Indians. It is usually dried and ground into blue cornmeal. We use coarsely ground blue cornmeal that is a blue-gray color ideal for fritters, muffins, and pancakes or as breading for vegetables. Blue cornmeal has an earthier flavor than white or yellow cornmeal, providing a characteristic flavor of desert cookery.

Chili Powder

Most of the many commercial chili powders available on the market today are blends of dried ground chili peppers, herbs, and spices. They vary in flavor and heat so it is best to experiment and find the brand you prefer. We use Santa Cruz chili powder, which is manufactured in Tumacacori, Arizona, about fifty miles south of us. This is a pure blend of chilies with no other spices or herbs added. I prefer it because it provides an assertive background flavor that I can modify by adding other ingredients.

Dried Corn Husks

Dried corn husks are available to us locally in supermarkets and specialty stores. With the increasing popularity of southwestern foods, they are also becoming available in specialty stores everywhere. Traditionally, corn husks are soaked in water to make them pliable and wrapped around tamales for steaming. We use them similarly to wrap and grill cabrilla, which takes on some of the corn flavor. Corn husks can also make attractive containers for salsas, relishes, and guacamole or they can be tied and placed under grilled fish, meat, or poultry.

Jícama

Jícama is a tuber with a thick, leathery brown skin covering a crunchy, moist, sweet meat. Its cool, refreshing flavor and high moisture content make it an ideal component in dishes needing a balance for fiery chilies. Jícama is also wonderful in salads, in a crudité basket, or alone with a squeeze of lime.

Tomatillos

This distinctive green vegetable native to Mexico is often mistaken for a green tomato when it is peeled of its papery husk. The fruit is round, about the size of a lime, and quite tart. It can be roasted to bring out some sweetness, chopped raw for salsas, or cooked in chutneys and sauces. As a vegetable, it can be sliced, coated with blue cornmeal, and pan-fried.

Cilantro

Sometimes called Mexican parsley, perhaps for its ubiquitousness in some Mexican cooking, this herb is a basic ingredient in southwestern cooking. It is a light green, leafy herb with thin spindly stems. Perishable, it is best stored refrigerated in water. Its unique, somewhat grassy, musty taste brings a characteristic flavor to salsas, soups, and pastas.

Basic Cooking Techniques

COOKING IS ESSENTIALLY THE PROCESS of building a dish one step at a time. Even the most elaborate recipes follow a logical progression. The key to executing recipes is to understand what the final product should be and the steps it will take to make it, and then to organize in advance all the equipment and ingredients you will need.

All of the recipes in this book can be accomplished by mastering a few fundamental cooking techniques. The methods we use are neither esoteric nor difficult. Many of them are basic to many styles of cooking.

SOUTHWESTERN TECHNIQUES

Some of the cooking methods we use, although not exclusive to the Southwest, are extremely common here. The techniques themselves help define the cuisine.

Grilling

Grilling is a technique as old as the fire over which primitive humans cooked their food. Centuries ago we put a grate over the flame to use as a cooking platform, and we haven't done much to improve the technique since.

Grilling is particularly popular in the Southwest, where hot summers and mild winters make cooking outdoors a year-round activity. At the restaurant, we cook indoors over a gas grill and outdoors over hardwoods such as mesquite or hickory that give distinct flavors to hearty foods. I prefer using gas indoors because it is cleaner to work with and does not impart too strong a flavor to more delicate fish and vegetables.

I write lots of grilled items into my menus because I love their clean, primitive simplicity and the wholesome outdoor flavor grilling imparts to food. I especially enjoy combining simple grilled foods with sophisticated French sauces. There is nothing better than king salmon hot off the grill served on a rich lobster sauce sprinkled with a confetti of sweet corn and roasted chilies and garnished with freshly picked squash blossom stuffed with scallop mousse. This dish combines the relative roughness of grilling with the refinement of a French sauce and light mousse to make a delicious and well-balanced main course.

The rules of grilling are as simple as the technique is pure. When cooking over hardwood or charcoal, let your coals burn to an ashen white. They are ready for cooking when the heat is too intense for you to hold your hand six inches above the grill. When cooking with gas, allow sufficient time for the grill to come completely to temperature. Regardless of the fuel source, be certain that the grill itself is clean and lightly oiled. This will prevent your food from sticking. I like to dip items into a mixture of salt, pepper, garlic, and olive oil before grilling them.

Test for doneness by touch and sight or, if you are unsure of your instincts, by using an instant thermometer. The cooking times given in recipes should be used only as a rough guide. Actual cooking times will vary with the fuel source, degree of heat, distance of the food from the fire, thickness of the food, and degree of doneness you prefer. Foods can be kept warm at the bottom or edges of the grill while you assemble the other components of your meal.

Smoking

Smoking was originally developed to preserve meat and fowl. Food to be smoked would be dried, cured in either a dry cure or brine, and cold-smoked for days, a process that retarded decay while flavoring the food. At the restaurant, our goal in smoking is not so much to preserve as to flavor, and our methods have been adapted accordingly.

When we first started smoking, our repertoire was limited to meat and fish. As we began to master the medium we experimented with more foods and now are successful with veal, poultry, vegetables, game, sausage, and pork. We have even smoked oysters and mussels for use in pasta dishes.

Smoking imparts a robust, woody flavor that can be subtle or strong depending on the type of wood used and the skill of the cook in manipulating the various elements of the process. There are basically two smoking processes, hot and cold. Hot smoking, the method we use, involves smoking over a small heat source in which the food cooks as it smokes and retains a good deal of its moisture. Hot smoking can be accomplished with very limited equipment. We find Weber kettles are perfect for our needs because they are durable and have tight-fitting lids and easily controllable drafts. Cold smoking requires a more elaborate setup in which the heat source is separate from the smoking chamber and the smoke itself is channeled into the chamber by tubing, drafts, or baffles. Cold smoking is a longer process than hot because it completely dries the food as it smokes. As moisture is removed, the food is permeated with smoke, resulting in a dried, highly flavored, preserved product.

CURING   The first step in the smoking process is to cure the food to be smoked. Curing is a means of drawing moisture from food for the purpose of drying it and facilitating the absorption of smoke and flavor. Cures can either be brines in which the product is immersed before smoking or dry cures which are rubbed into the flesh. Both types are made with high concentrations of salt in order to draw out moisture and allow smoke and flavor to be absorbed. Brines, which permeate the flesh more effectively, result in a drier product and are commonly used in cold smoking. Dry cures coat the surface and do not penetrate as deeply into the flesh as do brines. Dry cures yield a moister product that is strongly flavored on the surface.

BUILDING THE FIRE   We use a Weber kettle which we start with six to eight charcoal briquets. Once the briquets have turned to ash, we cover them with wet wood chips. (We store wood chips in buckets of water so they are always ready to use.) The wet chips smoulder over the fire and produce the volumes of smoke we need. For foods that take a long time to smoke, for instance brisket or prime rib, it is necessary to add additional briquets and chips to sustain the fire.

SMOKING CHART

Item	Curing	Type of Wood	Smoking Time
Beef Brisket (6 to 8 pounds)	12 to 24 hours	Mesquite or hickory	About 12 hours or until meat is tender; or braise brisket for 3 hours and, without curing, smoke for about 2 hours
Beef or pork ribs	12 to 24 hours	Mesquite or hickory	2 hours
New York strip (10 to 12 pounds)	12 to 24 hours	Mesquite or hickory	About 5 hours
Prime rib of beef	24 to 36 hours	Mesquite or hickory	Smoke about 4 hours, then finish in oven
Boneless veal loin	1 hour	Mesquite, cherry, or hickory	About 1½ hours
Duck breast	See recipes	Hickory	About 1 hour
Salmon	4 to 8 hours	Hickory, cherry, or alderwood	About 45 minutes
Shrimp	No cure	Mesquite, cherry, or hickory	About 15 minutes
Sea scallops	No cure	Cherry	5 to 10 minutes
Oysters in the shell	No cure	Mesquite or hickory	Until they open
Mussels in the shell	No cure	Mesquite or hickory	Until they open
Vegetables	No cure	Mesquite or hickory	Until they are soft

TIMING   There are four rules of thumb in deciding how long a food should be smoked:

- *For food to be served cold.* Smoke it to the degree of doneness you prefer. For example, if you like your meat medium rare, smoke it to medium rare.

- *For food to be served reheated.* Smoke it one degree less than you like it to be served; it will come up to temperature when reheated.

- *For food to be served directly from the smoke.* Smoke it to the degree of doneness you prefer.

- *For vegetables.* Smoke them until they soften but are still al dente.

Roasting Peppers

Peppers are roasted to remove their tough, waxy outer skin. There are different ways to accomplish this. In the restaurant we place the peppers directly over the open flames on the gas stove and turn them frequently until all sides are evenly and completely charred. We then submerge them in ice water to shock them, thereby loosening the skin and terminating the cooking process. It is then easy to peel the peppers under running water, exposing their bright, tender meat. Finally we remove the seeds and process them for specific recipes.

Peeling and Seeding Chilies

An easy way to peel chilies is to submerge them in hot oil. Heat two or three inches of vegetable oil in a deep-sided skillet until it starts to smoke and to spit when a drop of water is splashed into it. As with the peppers, have a bowl of ice water ready when you begin blistering the chilies. Submerge the chilies in the oil, working with long tongs to prevent burns from hot oil splatters. The skin will begin to blister immediately and will be completely blistered in less than a minute. Quickly transfer the chilies to the ice bath, where they will cool and their skin will loosen so that they are easy to peel. Chilies to be chopped should be peeled and seeded and their stems removed.

To prepare chilies for stuffing requires a little more care. First peel the chili, then carefully cut a slit down one side and delicately remove the seed pod, leaving the chili otherwise intact. You will use the stem for dipping the chili into batter when you make *chiles rellenos*.

Extracting Juice from Prickly Pears

Working with prickly pears is tricky because their stickers are sharp and insidious. We always use tongs and sometimes wear gloves. It is very important to clean your work place and tools thoroughly afterwards in order to prevent an errant sticker from turning up in your hand, or worse yet, in other food you might be preparing.

We use three different methods for extracting the juice, depending on the amount of prickly pears we're processing:

- *For small quantities.* You will need a cutting board, tongs, a knife, and a spoon. Cut the prickly pears in half lengthwise and scoop out the pulp and the seeds. Put pulp and seeds in a saucepan with a little water and cook them down. Strain liquid through double layers of cheesecloth to remove seeds and any stickers.

- *For larger quantities.* Chop the prickly pears and roughly purée them in a food processor or blender. Strain the juice twice through double layers of cheesecloth to be certain that all the stickers have been removed. Clean your equipment carefully.

- *For really large batches.* Roughly chop the prickly pears and simmer them in a large stockpot with enough water to cover. Boil fruit for about 3 hours; it should be quite soft. Then strain it twice through double layers of cheesecloth. Clean your pot thoroughly. Return syrup to pot and reduce it to evaporate the water and concentrate the flavor.

STANDARD TECHNIQUES

The recipes in this book make use of a few standard cooking techniques that are simple and require no special equipment.

Braising

Braising is a method generally reserved for tougher, less expensive cuts of meat. First the meat is seared to seal in its flavor; then it is cooked slowly in a covered pan with enough liquid such as stock or wine to come about halfway up the meat. We also use this method on tender meat, fish, or fowl when we want a food with crisp skin that has still absorbed the flavor of its braising liquid, for instance Burgundian Braised Beef Tenderloin.

Poaching

In poaching, the food is slowly simmered in a flavored liquid. As this is a gentle cooking method, it is commonly used with fish or poultry. The poached item takes on some of the flavor of the poaching liquid, producing a delicate, subtle dish.

Sautéing

In sautéing, the food is cooked quickly in a pan over high heat with a minimum of oil. The sauté pan must be very clean and coated with a thin layer of oil (optional in nonstick pans) to prevent sticking. Preheat the pan thoroughly before carefully placing the food into it. During the cooking the pan must be kept in constant motion so that the food cooks evenly without sticking or burning. Sauté pans have gently sloped sides that allow their contents to be easily flipped with just the flick of a wrist, a motion that becomes second nature with practice.

Clarifying Butter

Clarified butter is an easily made all-purpose cooking oil with a high smoking point. Starting with raw butter, simply melt the butter, skimming off the fat from the top. Then pour off the oil and discard the milk solids that will have settled to the bottom.

Blanching Vegetables

We typically serve anywhere from eight to fourteen fresh vegetables with our meals each night. If we were to try to cook all of these to order, accounting for the specific cooking times required for each, our nightly service would be a true nightmare. Instead, all vegetables requiring more than a minute are cooked in advance using a technique called blanching. First the vegetables are carved into the shapes we want, then they are either steamed or boiled in salted water. They are slightly undercooked at this point, and to stop the cooking they are submerged in ice water, drained, and refrigerated until needed. When we are ready to use them, we finish the cooking process by simmering them in seasoned stock or sautéing or grilling them—whatever is appropriate to the recipe.

Peeling and Seeding Tomatoes

Many of my recipes call for peeling, seeding, and chopping tomatoes. In France, tomato prepared in this way is known as *concassée*. To accomplish this easy technique, bring a pot of water to a vigorous boil and have a bowl of ice water ready as well. Remove the core from the tomato and score the other end with a shallow cross. Plunge the tomato into the boiling water for a minute or less, just until the skin appears to be loosening. Immediately transfer the tomato to the ice water to stop the cooking and make it cool enough to handle. You will now be able to peel the skin right off. Cut the tomato in half at the equator and gently squeeze out the seeds, poking and scooping with your fingers as needed. The tomato is now ready for chopping.

Sauces

WHETHER IT IS a cilantro aïoli swirled over pan-fried sweetbreads, a hearty purée of peppers spread under grilled beef tenderloin, or a suave beurre blanc infused with lobster stock and served under grilled king salmon, sauces always add an element of enchantment and sophistication. At Janos, we use a sauce to contrast with and complement other flavors and as a catalyst to unify distinct tastes into a coherent, well-balanced dish.

In the classical French tradition, many of our hot sauces are based on long-simmered stocks; others are made by cooking and puréeing fruits and vegetables. For cold sauces we use vinaigrettes, compound butters, purées of fruit, and emulsified egg sauces such as mayonnaise.

Stocks are basic to three general types of sauces we make: reduction sauces, cream sauces, and butter sauces. These all begin with the reduction of an appropriate stock. Reduction, a process of fortifying and thickening by simmering and resultant evaporation, is an important principle in our cooking because it gives sauces their richness and velvety consistency. Because we use reductions, we don't need to add roux, cornstarch, or other thickening agents, which tend to make sauces heavier and mask flavors as they thicken.

Pink peppercorn sauce, which we pair with lightly sautéed slices of veal, is a good example of our reduction technique. We start by sautéing sliced mushrooms with shallots and a little garlic, then flaming the mixture with brandy, sprinkling it with pink peppercorns, and reducing it with white wine. This provides the base for a sauce. The reduction of wine helps take the bite from the brandy, adding a bit of sweetness and a hint of citrus. If we were to add cream at this point the sauce would be satisfying, but it would lack richness and sophistication. The next step, then, is to add veal stock, which we reduce to a gloss. The stock unifies all of the flavors in a rich and body-giving cloak. The final step is to introduce heavy cream, which is in turn reduced, yielding a complex sauce spicy from the peppercorns and brandy, mellow from the mushrooms, rich with veal stock, and sophisticated with the final reduction of cream.

STOCKS

Reduced stocks are the foundation for almost all of our hot savory sauces. (Stocks are also good for enhancing flavor in purées.) We routinely make five different stocks: veal, chicken, fish, lobster, and duck. In addition, we sometimes make stocks from lamb, rabbit, and crayfish when we are cooking with these ingredients.

In their simplest form, stocks are made by slowly simmering bones or shells in water with a *mirepoix* (a mixture of diced aromatic vegetables), a sachet of herbs and spices, and for some stocks, wine and liquor. The recipes that follow specify ingredients, methods, and cooking times for each stock, but for all the general procedure is the same. Stocks can be made in advance, although fish and poultry stocks are more perishable than meat stocks. All of our stocks can be frozen with excellent success. Freezing stock is a good practice for the home cook because it allows stock to be prepared infrequently in quantities large enough for many recipes. Freeze the stock in quantities appropriate to the recipes you expect to make so that you only have to thaw what you will need.

Veal Stock

Makes 2 gallons

Have your butcher split the veal shank bones for you. This is important so that the gelatin is exposed and a thicker stock can be made. Splitting bones is easy for a butcher with a band saw but difficult and dangerous to attempt at home.

20 pounds split veal shank bones

3 heads celery, roughly chopped

7 large yellow onions, roughly chopped

10 large carrots, roughly chopped

1 cup (8 ounces) tomato paste

Preheat oven to 450°.

Put bones and vegetables in a roasting pan and roast them in oven for about 1½ hours, turning frequently, until bones are well browned. Transfer bones to a large stockpot, add tomato paste, and cover bones with cold water. Bring to a boil, then reduce heat and cook at a slow, rolling simmer for 48 hours, skimming off any foam that forms on the surface. Replace evaporated liquid with cold water as needed to keep bones covered.

Strain stock through a strainer layered with damp cheesecloth, pressing on bones and vegetables to extract their juices. Cool stock and reserve enough for immediate use, freezing remainder in small usable amounts.

Chicken Stock

Makes 2 gallons

15 pounds chicken backs or carcasses

2 heads celery, roughly chopped

4 large yellow onions, roughly chopped

6 large carrots, roughly chopped

Combine all ingredients in a large stockpot and cover with cold water. Bring to a boil, then reduce heat and cook at a slow rolling simmer for 5 to 6 hours, skimming off any foam that forms on the surface. Strain through a strainer layered with damp cheesecloth, pressing bones and vegetables to extract their juices. Cool stock and reserve enough for immediate use, freezing remainder in small usable batches.

Fish Stock

Makes 2 gallons

15 pounds fish bones from white fish such as halibut, cabrilla, or sole
2 heads celery, roughly chopped
4 large yellow onions, roughly chopped
6 large carrots, roughly chopped

Combine all ingredients in a large stockpot and cover with cold water. Bring to a boil then reduce heat and cook at a slow rolling simmer for 3 to 4 hours, skimming off any foam that forms on the surface. Strain through a strainer layered with damp cheesecloth, pressing bones and vegetables to extract their juices. Cool stock and reserve enough for immediate use, freezing remainder in small usable batches.

Lobster Stock

Makes 2 quarts

We make a batch of lobster stock every week or so when we have accumulated enough lobster, shrimp, and crayfish shells for a full recipe. You can do this at home with the smaller quantities listed here, or it may be practical for you to buy shrimp and lobster just for this purpose. Another option is to ask your fish supplier to save cooked lobster bodies for you, which should provide a substantial savings over live lobster.

2 pounds lobster shells *or*
   1 pound fresh lobster
2 pounds shrimp shells *or*
   1 pound fresh shrimp
2 pounds crayfish bodies *or*
   1 pound fresh crayfish
   (optional—if not available
   use 3 pounds each lobster
   and shrimp shells *or*
   1½ pounds each of the
   fresh shellfish)
2 pounds fish bones such as
   sole, halibut, or cabrilla,
   chopped
Olive oil for coating stockpot
4 carrots, roughly chopped
4 onions, roughly chopped
2 heads celery, roughly
   chopped
2 leeks, roughly chopped
6 tablespoons chopped
   garlic
1 cup tomato paste
2 cups brandy
8 cups (2 quarts) dry white
   wine
8 cups (2 quarts) water
¼ cup cracked black
   peppercorns
½ cup dried tarragon
12 whole cloves

In a food processor or blender or with a meat hammer, pulverize shells and fish bones to extract their juices. Heat a large stockpot with a thin coating of olive oil. Add pulverized shells and bones and all their juices. Stir constantly as shells cook and turn orange. This will take about 5 minutes.

Add carrots, onions, celery, leeks, garlic, tomato paste, and brandy. Flame brandy by igniting it with a match; shake pot vigorously to avoid scorching the shells. When flames subside, add wine, water, peppercorns, tarragon, and cloves and bring contents to a boil. Simmer for 3 hours. Strain through damp cheesecloth, pressing on shells to extract their juices, and reduce to 2 quarts.

Jus de Moules (Mussel Liquid)

Makes 4 cups

Jus de Moules is a versatile broth that can be served simply with the mussels it cooks with, combined with saffron and tomato to form a base for soups and stews, or reduced to provide a foundation for a more complex sauce. The mussels can be used immediately or reserved either in or out of the shell for a different dish such as a mussel and artichoke pithiviers.

1 yellow onion, roughly chopped
1 leek, cleaned and roughly chopped
2 carrots, roughly chopped
3 tablespoons chopped garlic
Salt and freshly ground pepper to taste
10 cups (2½ quarts) dry white wine
3 pounds fresh mussels, cleaned and mulched

Cover onion, leek, carrots, garlic, salt, and pepper with wine and reduce to 4 cups. Add mussels and cook covered for 3 to 5 minutes, until mussels have opened completely. Remove mussels and reserve them for another use. Strain broth and correct seasoning with additional salt and pepper if needed.

NOTE: Mulch mussels by covering them with water and ½ cup cornmeal and soaking them overnight in the refrigerator. This will cleanse them of any sand or grit.

Duck Stock

Makes 2 gallons

6 carcasses from roasted or
  butchered ducks
4 large yellow onions,
  roughly chopped
2 heads celery, roughly
  chopped
6 large carrots, roughly
  chopped
4 heads garlic, peeled and
  roughly chopped
Salt to taste
4 tablespoons cracked black
  peppercorns

Preheat oven to 450°.

Put carcasses and vegetables in a roasting pan and roast in oven for about 50 minutes, turning frequently until bones are well browned. Transfer bones and vegetables to a large stockpot and cover with cold water. Add salt and peppercorns. Bring to a boil, then reduce to a slow, rolling simmer and cook for 6 hours, skimming off any foam that forms on the surface. Replace evaporated liquid with cold water as needed to keep bones covered.

Strain stock through a strainer layered with damp cheesecloth, pressing on bones and vegetables to extract their juices. Degrease stock by skimming the fat from the top. Measure out enough for immediate use, and freeze remainder in small usable batches.

Lamb Stock

Makes 2 gallons

20 pounds trimmed lamb
  bones, split into small
  pieces
7 large yellow onions,
  roughly chopped
3 heads celery, roughly
  chopped
8 large carrots, roughly
  chopped
3 tablespoons kosher salt
4 tablespoons cracked black
  peppercorns

Preheat oven to 450°.

Put bones and vegetables in a roasting pan and roast them in oven for about 1½ hours, turning frequently, until bones are well browned. Transfer bones and vegetables to a large stockpot, add salt and pepper, and cover with cold water. Bring to a boil then reduce heat and cook at a slow, rolling simmer for about 24 hours, skimming off any foam that forms on the surface. Replace evaporated liquid with cold water as needed to keep bones covered.

Strain the stock through a strainer layered with damp cheesecloth, pressing on bones and vegetables to extract their juices. Degrease by skimming fat from the top. Reserve enough stock for immediate use, and freeze the remainder in small usable amounts.

REDUCTION SAUCES

Reduction sauces derive their flavor primarily from the stock from which they are made. They are relatively easy to prepare because they require few steps other than simmering excellent stock to a shiny, viscous glaze. Some of these sauces use liquor or wine as complementary flavors. Others use vegetables such as shallots, garlic, and mushrooms. In any case the resulting sauce will never be any better than its components, so great care must be taken in selecting ingredients. We serve most of our reduction sauces with veal or beef. Their intense flavors and relative lightness make a perfect complement for grilled meats, which are hearty enough to stand up to a fortified sauce.

One hint about reductions that will save you time: Use a large, flat sauté pan rather than a saucepan. The sauce will reduce much more quickly because there is more surface area to evaporate.

Burgundy Sauce

Makes 2 cups

6 cups (1½ quarts) Veal Stock (page 42)
4 cups (1 quart) good-quality burgundy wine
3 tablespoons chopped shallots
3 tablespoons chopped garlic

Combine all ingredients in a noncorrosive stockpot, bring to a boil, and continue cooking over high heat until reduced to 2 cups—approximately 2 hours. Strain through a strainer layered with damp cheesecloth.

Ginger Port Sauce

Makes 1 cup

This sauce is excellent with grilled beef tenderloin.

3 cups Veal Stock (page 42)
1 cup tawny port
2 tablespoons chopped
   ginger

Reduce stock by half. Add port and ginger and reduce to 1 cup. Strain out ginger and serve warm.

Truffled Port Sauce

Makes 2 cups

3 tablespoons chopped
   shallots
3 tablespoons chopped
   garlic
½ cup brandy
4 cups (1 quart) port
4 cups (1 quart) Veal Stock
   (page 42)
4 ounces truffles, chopped (if
   canned truffles are used,
   save juice)

In a heavy medium sauce pot, combine shallots and garlic over high heat, shaking pot to prevent scorching. Add brandy and, when warm, ignite with a match. When flames subside, add port, stock, three-fourths of truffles, and any truffle juice. Bring to a boil and cook over high heat until reduced to 2 cups. Strain through a fine mesh strainer and add remaining truffles as garnish.

New Mexico Red Chili Sauce

Makes 3 cups

This is one of our more complex reduced sauces. It combines the south-western flavors of chilies and chocolate with a sophisticated reduction of Veal Stock. Red chili sauce is quite hot and must be paired with a forceful dish such as Spicy Lamb Tamales.

½ pound dried pasilla chilies, chopped and stems
   removed (ancho chilies
   may be substituted)
10 cups (2½ quarts) Veal
   Stock (page 42)
3 Anaheim chilies, chopped
2 poblano chilies, chopped
2 onions, chopped
4 tablespoons chopped
   garlic
2 tablespoons clarified butter
4 sticks cinnamon
2 tablespoons whole cloves
½ cup fresh lime juice
2 ounces semisweet chocolate, grated
Salt and freshly ground pepper to taste

Simmer pasilla chilies in half the stock for about 20 minutes, until they are quite soft. Purée mixture and reserve.

Sauté Anaheim chilies, poblano chilies, onions, and garlic in clarified butter until they soften, about 5 minutes. Add remaining stock, cinnamon, cloves, and lime juice and bring to a boil.

To this second mixture add the purée of pasilla chilies. Continue boiling until reduced to 3 cups; this will take approximately 1½ hours. Strain sauce through a fine mesh strainer. Stir in chocolate and season with salt and pepper.

Prickly Pear Compote

Makes 2 cups

Every year, prickly pear compote first appears on our menus in mid-August when the fruit begins to ripen on the cactus in my yard at home. How to make the syrup is described in "Basic Cooking Techniques." I understand that prickly pear syrup is available commercially as well. Although I can't vouch for the product personally, you may want to try it if you aren't lucky enough to have access to the raw fruit.

Clarified butter
1 yellow onion, medium diced
2 Anaheim chilies, peeled, seeded (see page 34 for directions), and medium diced
1 teaspoon chopped garlic
3 tablespoons fine-julienne-cut sun-dried tomatoes
4 tablespoons kernels from 1 small ear sweet corn
3 tablespoons cooked Black Beans (page 198)
Salt and freshly ground pepper to taste
1 cup prickly pear syrup
3 tablespoons fresh lime juice
2 cups Veal Stock (page 42)

In a large sauté pan, heat enough clarified butter to coat pan and sauté onion until almost translucent. Add chilies and garlic and sauté 1 minute longer. Add tomatoes, corn, beans, salt, and pepper and stir vigorously to combine all ingredients. Add prickly pear syrup, lime juice, and stock, bring to a boil, and reduce to 2 cups, stirring constantly to avoid scorching.

CREAM SAUCES

Cream sauces are essentially reductions that have been enriched by the addition and reduction of heavy cream. The cream ennobles a sauce with luxuriousness while acting as a subtle bond to pull together disparate flavors into a unified dish. We normally use manufacturer's cream because it is heavier and thicker than whipping cream and yields a richer sauce (though for the home cook, whipping cream gives quite satisfactory results). Sometimes we substitute crème fraîche or sour cream when we desire a slight tartness. We always reduce the cream by twenty-five to forty percent in order to intensify its flavor and thicken the sauce so that it will coat rather than be soupy.

Cream sauces can be more complex than straight reduction sauces, which tend to rely on the interplay of relatively few ingredients. The cream provides a neutral background that can support a variety of flavors and scents, allowing them to coalesce into an exciting, unified whole. The amount of cream in a sauce is somewhat subjective. In my recipes I have called for the amount that provides the ratio of cream to reduced stock to liquid that I like. How much cream you decide to use may be based on dietary considerations as well as taste. All of my sauces will be flavorful and will complement your food well with less cream, but they will also be less rich, and in some cases less unified. For those watching their cholesterol levels, the reduction sauces and purées can be appropriate substitutes.

Lobster Sauce

Makes 2 cups

¼ cup chopped shallots
¼ cup chopped garlic
6 tablespoons brandy
2 tablespoons anisette
2 cups Lobster Stock (page 44)
2 cups heavy cream
Salt and freshly ground pepper to taste

In a heavy medium sauce pot, combine shallots and garlic over high heat, shaking pot to prevent them from burning. Add brandy and anisette and, when warm, ignite with a match. When flames subside, add stock and reduce to 1 cup. Add cream and reduce to 2 cups. Strain through a fine mesh strainer and season with salt and pepper.

Roasted Garlic Sauce

Makes 2 cups

6 heads garlic, unpeeled and roasted whole until soft throughout (about 1 hour at 325°)
2 cups dry white wine
6 tablespoons chopped shallots
½ cup fresh lime juice
2 cups Chicken Stock (page 42) (or use Fish Stock if sauce is to be served with seafood)
2 cups heavy cream
Salt and freshly ground pepper to taste

Slice garlic heads in half and squeeze cloves from their skins into a noncorrosive stockpot. Add wine, shallots, and lime juice and bring to a boil. Continue cooking until liquid is reduced to ½ cup. Add stock and reduce to 1 cup. Add cream and reduce to 2 cups. Strain through a fine mesh strainer and season with salt and pepper.

With Dana Smithson at K and D Greenhouse

With sous-chef Neal Swidler

Picking prickly pears with Ben

Prickly pear cactus fruit

Sweet Corn Chowder Sauce

Makes 2 cups

4 ounces smoked bacon, diced (preferably mesquite-smoked but hickory is fine too)
½ large yellow onion, medium diced
1 tablespoon chopped garlic
¾ cup dry white wine
½ cup Mussel Liquid (page 45) (clam juice may be substituted)
Kernels from 1 ear sweet corn
1 cup heavy cream
1 small new red potato, peeled, diced, and steamed until soft but still firm
2 medium tomatoes, skinned, seeded, and chopped
Salt and freshly ground pepper to taste

In a sauté pan, cook bacon over low heat to render fat; pour off excess grease. Add onion and sauté with bacon until translucent. Add garlic, wine, Mussel Liquid, and corn; reduce until ⅓ cup remains. Add cream and reduce by one-third. Finish by adding potato, tomato, salt, and pepper.

Mimosa Sauce

Makes 2 cups

I like to use this sauce for light fish such as grilled scallops, trout, and pompano.

1½ cups fresh orange juice
1½ cups champagne
¾ cup chopped shallots
2 cups heavy cream
Salt to taste

Combine orange juice, champagne, and shallots in a noncorrosive sauce pot and reduce to 1 cup. Add cream and reduce to 2 cups. Strain through a fine mesh strainer and season with salt.

Santa Cruz Chili Sauce

Makes 2 cups

This sauce is great by itself under a *chile relleno* or a grilled chicken breast or when simmered with Sweet Corn Salsa and served under a hickory-smoked veal loin.

3 tablespoons chopped garlic
1 yellow onion, medium diced
4 tablespoons Santa Cruz chili powder
4 tablespoons Santa Cruz chili paste
2 tablespoons cumin powder
3 cups Chicken Stock (page 42)
3 cinnamon sticks
4 tablespoons whole cloves
2 cups heavy cream
Salt and freshly ground pepper to taste

Sauté onions and garlic together until soft. Stir in chili powder, chili paste, and cumin and simmer briefly. Add stock, cinnamon sticks, and cloves and reduce to 1 cup. Add cream and reduce to 2 cups. Strain through a fine mesh strainer and season with salt and pepper.

Madeira Sauce

Makes 2 cups

2 tablespoons chopped garlic
2 tablespoons chopped shallots
2 cups Madeira wine
1 cup Chicken Stock (page 42)
1½ cups heavy cream
Salt and freshly ground pepper to taste

Combine garlic, shallots, Madeira, and stock, bring to a boil, and reduce to 1 cup, about 20 minutes. Add cream and reduce to 2 cups. Season with salt and pepper.

Marsala Sauce

Makes 1 cup

Clarified butter for sautéing
6 ounces domestic mushrooms, sliced
½ cup chopped scallions
½ tablespoon chopped garlic
¾ cup sweet Marsala wine
¾ cup Veal Stock (page 42)
¾ cup heavy cream
Salt and freshly ground pepper to taste

Over high heat, coat a medium sauté pan with clarified butter and sauté mushrooms, scallions, and garlic until they begin to soften, about 1 minute. Add Marsala and reduce to ⅓ cup. Add stock and reduce to ⅔ cup. Add cream and reduce to 1 cup. Season with salt and pepper.

Apple Cider Sauce

Makes 1 cup

¼ cup chopped shallots
¾ cup apple cider
¾ cup dry white wine
¾ cup heavy cream

In a medium sauce pot, combine shallots, cider, and wine, bring to a boil, and reduce to ½ cup. Add cream and reduce to 1 cup.

BUTTER SAUCES

The butter sauces we use fall into two categories—emulsified butter sauces, of which beurre blanc is the most common example, and butter-enhanced sauces, those finished with butter to provide a delicate, satisfying sheen. Emulsified butter sauces are made by whisking raw, softened butter into a reduced liquid, usually wine or vinegar. The flavor of the base or reduction should be quite intense because it will be mellowed by volumes of butter whipped into suspension. In these sauces the butter itself provides flavor as it balances the strong reduction. The magic of a beurre blanc sauce is that it is at once light and delicate and also rich and flavorful. This balance is accomplished by creating a strong emulsion when whipping the butter into the reduction. The whipping action molecularly suspends particles of the reduction in the volumes of butter, incorporating them throughout the sauce while linking them to the butter molecules. The resulting sauce has a mellow buttery flavor and a light, smooth texture. The strength and consistency of the sauce can be adjusted by varying the amount of butter.

Butter-enhanced sauces differ from beurre blancs in the role the butter is asked to play. In a butter-enhanced sauce, the butter is added at the end to an otherwise complete sauce. Its job is to thicken the sauce slightly, give it a richer, more rounded flavor, and provide it with a glossy polish. The butter itself does not give a strong flavor but rather enhances existing flavors. Whether to finish a sauce with butter is a matter of personal taste. As the sauce is otherwise complete, the butter adds a final dimension that you may not need or want. We finish with butter when we feel the flavors need rounding out, when a dish will benefit aesthetically from a satiny finish, or when the flavor of the dish will benefit from that final touch of butter. Not all sauces require or will be improved by butter. An already rich cream sauce may become unctuous if butter is added, a reduction sauce meant to be robust may become cloying and pretentious. Butter is just one element of many at the cook's disposal; it is rich and fattening and should be used judiciously.

In making butter sauces, proper technique is imperative. Improperly prepared butter sauces may fail to emulsify or may do so temporarily, only to separate when ladled onto a warm plate. The critical variable in both emulsified butter and butter-enhanced sauces is temperature. In either case, softened, room-temperature butter must be quickly whipped into liquid that has been simmered and removed from the heat. The butter should be whisked in bit by bit so as not to cool the sauce too quickly, which would make it impossible to incorporate all of the butter. When large quantities of beurre blanc sauce are made, requiring that large volumes of butter be added, the sauce can occasionally be returned to a low heat while the butter continues to be whisked in. If the liquid is too hot when the butter is introduced, the butter will melt, separating into its components of salt, fat, and milk. The butter must retain its structure in order to support an emulsion.

Once completed, these sauces are still sensitive to temperature. They can be held fairly warm either in a thermos or in a warm place in the kitchen. If the environment is too hot the sauce will separate. Care must also be taken with the temperature of the plate onto which the sauce will be ladled. If it is too hot, the sauce will separate; too cold and it will congeal. The plate should be warm to the touch. If it is too hot to grip, it is probably too hot for the sauce also.

Beurre Blanc

Makes 2 cups

2 cups dry white wine
3 tablespoons chopped garlic
3 tablespoons chopped shallots
1 tablespoon cream (optional)
8 ounces (2 sticks) butter at room temperature, cut into 1-ounce pieces

Combine wine, garlic, and shallots in a saucepan, bring to a boil, and reduce to ½ cup liquid. Add cream, if used; cream stabilizes the sauce and helps it hold under warmer temperatures. Remove reduction from heat and whisk in butter 1 piece at a time. Each piece should be three-fourths emulsified before the next is added. Store in a thermos or warm, but not hot, spot in the kitchen. Butter sauces cannot be reheated or they will separate.

VARIATIONS:

Cilantro-Tomato Beurre Blanc

Add 4 tablespoons skinned, seeded, and finely chopped tomato and 2 tablespoons roughly chopped cilantro leaves to the finished sauce.

Dill Beurre Blanc

Add 2 tablespoons fresh dill to the reducing liquid. Strain completed sauce and finish with 4 tablespoons roughly chopped dill. This method can be used with any fresh herb.

Lemon Beurre Blanc

Add ½ cup fresh lemon juice to the 2 cups white wine and proceed as for Beurre Blanc.

Lobster Beurre Blanc

Decrease amount of white wine to 1 cup, combine it with 2 cups Lobster Stock, and proceed as for Beurre Blanc.

Beurre Rouge

Makes 2 cups

Beurre Rouge is the same sauce as Beurre Blanc except that red wine is substituted for white. When used with meat, such as Grilled New York Strips Beurre Rouge and Chili Hollandaise, it's nice to reduce the red wine with equal parts of Veal Stock. The resulting sauce is stronger and meatier and goes well with a grilled steak. Similarly, when used with fish, such as Didier's Hawaiian Snapper, Mussel Liquid or Fish Stock can be reduced with the wine.

2 tablespoons chopped garlic

2 tablespoons chopped shallots

1 cup Veal Stock (page 42) (if sauce is to be served with meat) *or* (if sauce is to be served with fish) 1 cup Mussel Liquid (page 45), Fish Stock (page 43), or clam juice

1½ cups burgundy wine

8 ounces (2 sticks) butter at room temperature, cut into 1-ounce pieces

In stainless-steel sauce pot, combine all ingredients except butter. Reduce liquid to ½ cup. Remove from heat and briskly whip in butter 1 piece at a time. Each piece should be three-fourths emulsified before the next is added. Store in a thermos or in a warm, but not hot, place.

PURÉES

Puréeing is a primitive and simple technique of sauce making. Originally, vegetables or fruit were boiled to a pulp and forced through a strainer or food mill in order to render them smooth and homogeneous. This technique was, and still is, commonly employed to make soups or to make hard-to-chew foods easier to swallow. We use a food processor and strainer more often than a food mill because it is a quicker way to get the same results. We elevate the technique by infusing purées with stocks, liquors, and herbs to create sophisticated sauces; even then, however, the method is basically one of processing ingredients to a semiliquid form. We purée different ingredients together to obtain a smooth, flavorful base for sauces. We also purée fruit to be served either warm or cold with desserts or to be used as a base for other sauces.

Deciding whether to make a purée for a particular dish involves looking at the entire dish and its desired effect. Texture, flavor, and presentation are key considerations. For instance, when developing a sweetbread recipe for our fall menu one year, we discovered that sweetbreads and pumpkin were immensely satisfying together. The problem was how to combine them in a way that was sophisticated and attractive and that also allowed each ingredient to retain its integrity while blending well into a coherent dish. There were any number of options to try. We finally hit upon a purée of pumpkins, which we simmer in chicken stock and serve under the pan-fried sweetbreads. The flavor of the pumpkin is tempered by onion, carrot, and butter so that it doesn't overpower the subtle sweetbreads. The combination forms the core of a dish that is completed with a drizzle of Cilantro Aïoli and a sprinkling of crunchy candied pecans.

Purées of fruit can be used with entrées in a similar fashion as vegetables. When peaches start to come into season in the spring, I like to purée them for serving under hickory-smoked duck breast which is then napped with an anise-flavored, raspberry-enhanced butter sauce and dotted with spicy green peppercorns.

Pumpkin Purée

Makes 3 cups

1 pound pumpkin, seeded, peeled, and roughly chopped (acorn or butternut squash may be substituted)
1 yellow onion, peeled and roughly chopped
2 carrots, roughly chopped
6 cups (1½ quarts) Chicken Stock (page 42)
5 tablespoons butter at room temperature
Salt and freshly ground pepper to taste

Simmer squash, onions, and carrots in stock until vegetables are quite soft. Strain off stock and reserve for another use. In a food processor or blender, purée pumpkin and vegetables completely. Purée in butter and season with salt and pepper.

Roasted Pepper Purée

Makes 1 cup

3 red bell peppers, roasted, peeled, seeded (see page 34 for directions), and roughly chopped
3 green bell peppers, roasted, peeled, seeded, and roughly chopped
2 Anaheim chilies, peeled, seeded (see page 34 for directions), and roughly chopped
1 yellow onion, roughly chopped
2 tablespoons chopped garlic
1 cup Chicken Stock (page 42)
½ cup dry white wine
Salt and freshly ground pepper to taste
3 tablespoons butter at room temperature

In a food processor, purée peppers, chilies, onion, and garlic until smooth. Place purée in a large sauté pan with stock and wine, bring to a boil, and reduce until liquid is thick enough to coat the back of a spoon. Season with salt and pepper, remove from heat, and whisk in butter.

VARIATION:

This sauce is also wonderful served under grilled beef tenderloin. To adapt the sauce for beef, substitute Veal Stock for chicken and red wine for white. For our Medallions of Beef with Five Peppers, I like to stud the fillets with cracked black peppercorns before grilling and then sprinkle pink peppercorns over the finished sauce on the plate. To make an attractive garnish, reserve strips of the roasted peppers and crisscross them on top of the cooked medallions.

Peach Purée

This purée is delicious served with smoked duckling.

6 fresh peaches, peeled and
   stone removed
2 tablespoons brandy
3 tablespoons butter at room
   temperature

Purée all ingredients. To serve, gently heat the purée, whisking constantly to maintain the emulsion of butter and peach.

NOTE: To peel peaches, score their tops with an X using a sharp knife, and plunge them into boiling water for 30 seconds to loosen their skin. Then plunge them immediately into ice water. The skins will come right off. If you use freestone peaches, they can be easily split and the stone removed.

Mango Purée

For desserts or on a cooled Poached Salmon Salad.

2 large fresh mangos, peeled
   and pit removed
½ cup fresh lime juice

Purée mangos and lime juice, strain through fine strainer, and serve.

Raspberry Purée

3 cups fresh or frozen
   raspberries

Purée raspberries and strain.

EMULSIFIED SAUCES

Hollandaise is considered one of the four "mother" sauces of classical French cooking. From it we derive mayonnaise in all its forms, the emulsified butter sauces described earlier, emulsified vinaigrettes, the variously flavored hollandaise sauces, and their enriched cousin, mousseline. All of these sauces are based on emulsification, and many use egg yolks as a foundation into which melted butter or oil is whipped.

Hollandaise itself is the most difficult of these sauces to learn. Once the technique is mastered, the others will follow easily. Hollandaise is made by emulsifying clarified butter with cooked egg yolks. There are several key variables to control in this process:

1. The ratio of butter to cooked egg yolks is two ounces of butter to one large yolk. The egg yolk can support only a limited amount of butter. Too much and it will separate; too little and it will be weak and taste eggy.

2. The egg yolk must be cooked gently in a large stainless-steel bowl over low direct heat or on top of a water bath. The yolks must be kept in constant motion to avoid scorching. I like to work with a large balloon flex whip to create a light, fluffy texture. To aid their cooking we add a splash of white wine to the yolks. This introduces flavor and provides a medium in which the yolks can cook. They are finished cooking when they turn pale yellow and the wine has evaporated.

3. The butter should be warm but not hot. Too hot and it will curdle the eggs; too cold and it will congeal as it is whipped into the eggs. After the egg yolks have cooked, remove them from the heat and gradually whisk in the butter in a slow, steady stream.

4. The completed sauce must be held in a warm, not hot, environment. Like the butter sauces it will separate if it is too hot and congeal if too cold.

After it is completed the hollandaise is flavored with lemon juice, salt, and pepper. Some of the flavored derivative sauces, such as chili hollandaise, gain their distinctive flavor from substituting a reduction for the white wine that is cooked with the egg yolks. Other derivative sauces are based on the same techniques of emulsifying egg and oil (clarified butter being an oil) but differ from hollandaise and each other in the ratio of eggs to oil, the temperature at which they are prepared, and the additional flavors they use. The simplest of the variations is mousseline sauce, which is simply a hollandaise lightened and enriched by the addition of whipped cream folded into it. Mayonnaises and emulsified vinaigrettes are made at room temperature. They use raw eggs and will support a considerably higher ratio of oil to egg yolks. Temporarily emulsified vinaigrettes are made by whipping together oil and vinegar. The combination will separate quickly and needs to be rewhipped before each use.

Hollandaise

Makes 2 cups

3 egg yolks
¼ cup dry white wine
6 ounces (1½ sticks) butter, melted and held warm
1 tablespoon fresh lemon juice
Salt and white pepper to taste

In a large stainless-steel bowl, whisk together egg yolks and wine using a large balloon flex whip. Place bowl directly over a medium flame or, for slower but more certain results, over a double boiler. Whisk egg yolks, keeping them in constant motion so that they cook evenly and don't scorch. Yolks are cooked when they turn a pale yellow, thicken slightly, and the wine has evaporated.

Remove yolks from heat and whisk in butter 1 drop at a time to form a strong emulsion. As the process continues, butter can be added more quickly, but always make certain the emulsion is maintained. Season with lemon juice, salt, and pepper. You may hold sauce in a warm place until ready to use, but do not try to reheat it or it will separate.

VARIATIONS:

Lobster Hollandaise
Reduce 2 cups Lobster Stock to ¼ cup, and replace white wine with this reduction. After Hollandaise is complete, fold in 3 ounces finely diced lobster meat.

CONTINUED →

Mousseline Sauce

Mousseline is simply Hollandaise that has been lightened and enriched by the addition of whipped cream. We use Mousseline as a topping on Mussels Castroville or Asparagus Mousseline in Puff Pastry, where we want a lighter sauce that will brown but not crust over when gratinéed.

Whip 1 cup heavy cream to soft peaks and delicately fold it into the completed Hollandaise recipe.

Chili Hollandaise

Makes 1 cup reduction

Chili Hollandaise, a variation of classic hollandaise, was inspired by béarnaise sauce, itself a derivative of hollandaise. Béarnaise derives its characteristic flavor from a reduction of tarragon, chervil, and shallots. In Chili Hollandaise, we use a reduction of chilies, onions, garlic, and cracked peppercorns to give the hollandaise a distinctive southwestern flavor.

½ yellow onion, finely diced
2 tablespoons chopped garlic
1 tablespoon cracked black peppercorns
2 Anaheim chilies, peeled, seeded (see page 34 for directions), and finely diced
¼ teaspoon chiltepin or red pepper flakes
3 cups dry white wine
½ cup white wine vinegar

Combine all ingredients in a saucepan, bring to a boil, and reduce to 1 cup. To make Chili Hollandaise, replace the white wine in Hollandaise recipe with ¼ cup reduction and proceed as instructed there. Unused reduction can be saved in the refrigerator.

Mayonnaise

Makes 2 cups

Mayonnaise is the base for many other brightly flavored sauces, such as Cilantro Aïoli. My basic recipe differs from some you may have used. I like to include a little mustard and garlic for a bit of spiciness, a variation that isn't essential but is worth trying. If you like a lot of garlic, try my Garlic Aïoli, which has a pronounced garlic flavor.

4 egg yolks
1 teaspoon chopped garlic
1 teaspoon Pommeray or
    other whole-grain mustard
2 cups olive oil
Juice of 2 lemons
Salt and freshly ground pep-
    per to taste

In a food processor, thoroughly combine egg yolks, garlic, and mustard. With motor running, add oil in a very slow, steady stream so that it forms an emulsion with egg yolks. With motor still running, finish by adding lemon juice, salt, and pepper.

NOTE: Be careful not to overprocess the mayonnaise because the heat from the processor may break down the emulsion.

VARIATIONS:

Garlic Aïoli
Increase amount of garlic to 2 tablespoons.

Cilantro Aïoli
Purée 1 cup picked-over cilantro leaves with egg yolks, garlic, and mustard.

Red Pepper Aïoli
Add 1 cup puréed and strained red bell peppers to the completed mayonnaise.

Balsamic Vinaigrette

Makes 2 cups

This basic vinaigrette serves as the house dressing on the salads that accompany our dinners. I like it for the sweet, rich, yet slightly tart flavor that the balsamic vinegar provides. Tossed with a simple salad of crisp let-tuces it is wonderfully refreshing.

All of the vinaigrette recipes given in this book can be reduced or extended simply by adjusting the recipes to yield the amount you want. Don't worry if you end up with more dressing than you need. It will store indefinitely refrigerated in a sealed glass jar. Simply remix before each use.

1½ cups olive oil
½ cup balsamic vinegar

Combine oil and vinegar, mixing well to form a temporary emulsion.

Opal Basil Vinaigrette

Makes 2¾ cups

There are dozens of varieties of basil available from seed companies these days, each with its own distinctive flavor. Opal basil is dark purple and richer in flavor than the green basil commonly found in grocery stores. This recipe will be good with any basil you choose.

2 cups olive oil
1 tablespoon finely chopped garlic
1 cup opal basil, picked over and roughly chopped
¾ cup balsamic vinegar

In a large mixing bowl, whip oil into garlic and basil. Then slowly whip in vinegar to create a temporary emulsion.

Walnut Vinaigrette

Makes 2¾ cups

2 cups walnut oil
1 tablespoon finely chopped
    garlic
¾ cup balsamic vinegar

In a large mixing bowl whip oil into garlic. Then slowly whip in vinegar to create a temporary emulsion.

Sesame Dipping Sauce

Makes 2 cups

3 teaspoons ginger powder
3 teaspoons garlic powder
½ cup sesame oil
¼ cup soy sauce
¼ cup rice wine vinegar
¼ cup dry sherry
¾ cup granulated sugar (or
    more or less to taste)

In a medium stainless-steel bowl combine the ginger and garlic powder. Slowly pour in the sesame oil, working the dry ingredients into smooth paste. Proceed to whisk in remaining liquids slowly, one at a time, in order to maintain a temporary emulsion. Dissolve the sugar at the end and adjust the sweetness to your liking.

The sauce can hold indefinitely in the refrigerator; just make sure it is well mixed before serving.

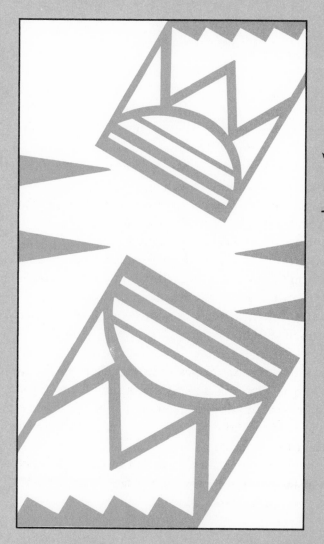

Salsas &
Pestos

*S*ALSAS MAY BE *the* characteristic note of Mexican cooking. Every Mexican restaurant in Tucson serves its own concoction with chips at the start of a meal. In Sonora and southern Arizona the salsas are primarily tomato-based. As you travel farther south in Mexico, other ingredients such as tomatillos and avocadoes are used as well.

Salsas range from mild to fiery-hot and can be a thin broth or a chunky substance like our own Salsa Fresca. Salsas are always used to complement foods and are often served separately to allow individual eaters to add as much or as little as they like. I have friends for whom a meal isn't complete if they don't put salsa on everything; others use salsa as a well-chosen accent. One of the great features about salsas is that they are generally low in cholesterol and relatively nonfattening. They are therefore a great substitute for rich sauces when your cooking needs a lot of flavor without a lot of calories.

We developed our salsa recipes as distinct elements for specific dishes. Because our cooking spans many styles and incorporates many ingredients and flavors, our salsa repertoire has to be equally diverse. The salsas we've introduced at Janos have been well received by local aficionados, who judged them Tucson's best in 1988.

This section includes recipes for pestos and a couple of condiments because in most instances they are used in the same way as salsas—to accent, complement, and complete dishes.

Salsa Fresca

Makes 3 cups

6 garden tomatoes, medium
   diced
½ red onion, finely diced
1 bunch scallions, finely
   diced
1 Anaheim chili, peeled,
   seeded (see page 34 for
   directions), and diced small
½ poblano chili, peeled,
   seeded, and diced small

1 bunch cilantro, roughly
   chopped
1 tablespoon finely chopped
   garlic
1 tablespoon balsamic
   vinegar
1 tablespoon red wine
   vinegar
1 tablespoon olive oil
Salt and freshly ground pepper to taste

Combine all ingredients and mix well.

Tomatillo Salsa

Makes 2 cups

12 tomatillos, husks removed
    and washed
1 whole onion
2 serrano chilies, seeded
1 tablespoon chopped garlic
2 bunches scallions, finely
   chopped
1 bunch cilantro, roughly
   chopped
1 tablespoon olive oil
Salt and pepper to taste

Roughly chop tomatillos, onion, and chilies, then coarsely purée them with garlic. Fold in scallions, cilantro, and oil. Season with salt and pepper.

Smoked Tomato Salsa

Makes 2 cups

After cooking elsewhere for several years, Neal Swidler took a cut in pay and position to come work for me as a dishwasher. He is now my sous-chef. One summer he came back from a vacation in Texas with the idea of using smoked tomatoes in a salsa. I consider the result to be one of our best salsas.

6 tomatoes, seeded, peeled, and chopped
2 tablespoons olive oil
1 medium yellow onion, diced
1 tablespoon chopped garlic
2 medium Anaheim chilies, peeled, seeded (see page 34 for directions), and diced
1 tablespoon fresh oregano *or* 2 teaspoons dried oregano leaves
½ cup red wine vinegar
Salt and freshly ground pepper to taste

Prepare a smoker using hickory wood.

To smoke tomatoes, create a container from a 12-by 12-inch square of aluminum foil with the sides folded up. Line container with parchment paper (otherwise acid in the tomatoes would eat through the foil). Poke holes in container to let smoke through and add tomatoes. Place container directly on smoker grill, cover smoker, and smoke for about 30 minutes.

Heat oil in a sauté pan and sauté onion, garlic, chilies, and oregano until onion is soft. Deglaze pan with vinegar. Add smoked tomatoes and simmer until liquid is reduced by two-thirds. Season with salt and pepper.

Sweet Corn Salsa

Makes 2 cups

This versatile salsa is the base for Bay Scallop Salsa and for Salsa Santa Cruz.

Kernels from 2 ears sweet
   corn
1 large red onion, diced
   small
2 large tomatoes, diced
   medium
1 large red bell pepper, diced
   small
1 large green bell pepper,
   diced small
1 tablespoon finely chopped
   garlic
Salt and freshly ground pepper to taste

Combine all ingredients and mix well.

Bay Scallop Salsa

Makes 2 cups

Both Bay Scallop Salsa and Salsa Santa Cruz differ from our other salsas in that they are served hot in either a broth or sauce rather than cold as a relish. They are really hybrids of salsas and sauces which I've included in the salsa category because their base of peppers, onions, and chilies is characteristic of salsas.

Try this Bay Scallop Salsa with grilled cabrilla.

1 cup Sweet Corn Salsa
   (page 73)
½ cup dry white wine
4 ounces fresh bay scallops
4 tablespoons cooked Black
   Beans (page 198)
2 tablespoons butter at room
   temperature

Combine Sweet Corn Salsa and wine in a saucepan and simmer for 3 minutes. Add scallops and simmer an additional 2 minutes. Stir in beans. Remove from heat and whisk in butter until emulsified.

Salsa Santa Cruz

Makes 2 cups

Salsa Santa Cruz is a variation of Bay Scallop Salsa that emphasizes the hearty aspects of the black beans, corn, and chilies by simmering them with Santa Cruz Chili Sauce. The result is a full-bodied sauce that is excellent with veal or beef.

Clarified butter for sautéing
¼ cup onion, medium diced
¼ cup red bell pepper, medium diced
¼ cup green bell pepper, medium diced
1 Anaheim chili, peeled, seeded (see page 34 for directions), and medium diced
1 teaspoon chopped garlic
Salt and freshly ground black pepper to taste
1½ cups Santa Cruz Chili Sauce (page 54)
Kernels from 1 small ear sweet corn
⅓ cup cooked and drained Black Beans (page 198)

In a large saucepan, heat enough butter to coat pan and briefly sauté onion, peppers, and chili with garlic, salt, and pepper. Add Santa Cruz Chili Sauce, corn, and beans and simmer until reduced to 2 cups liquid.

VARIATION:

Substitute New Mexico Red Chili Sauce for Santa Cruz Chili Sauce. This makes a peppier salsa ideal for serving with Pork and Pepito Tamales.

Avocado Papaya Salsa

Makes 2 cups

3 papayas, peeled, seeded, and diced large
3 Haas avocadoes, peeled, seeded, and diced large
3 tablespoons red onion, finely diced
⅛ teaspoon chiltepin or red pepper flakes
3 tablespoons fresh lime juice
3 tablespoons sour cream

Gently combine all ingredients. If not to be used immediately, cover and refrigerate. In any case use within 2 hours since the salsa will begin to break up after that.

Mango Salsa

Makes 2 cups

3 mangos, peeled, seeded, and diced large
3 tablespoons finely diced red onion
1 poblano chili, peeled, seeded (see page 34 for directions), and finely diced
2 tablespoons fresh lime juice
1 bunch cilantro, finely chopped
Salt to taste

Immediately before serving, combine all ingredients, and mix well.

Basil Pesto

Makes 2 cups

This recipe can be made with any variety of basil with very interesting results. We've used lemon basil, opal basil, and cinnamon basil to create unusual flavorings for pastas, stuffings, and sauces. Because pesto freezes so well, we take advantage of its abundance during the summer to make numerous batches and freeze them for later use.

¾ cup (6 ounces) pine nuts (blanched almonds may be substituted)

3 tablespoons chopped garlic

12 ounces fresh basil

4 ounces Parmesan cheese, grated

Salt and freshly ground pepper to taste

½ cup olive oil

1 tablespoon fresh lemon juice

In a food processor fitted with a stainless-steel blade, finely grind nuts and garlic. Add basil, cheese, salt, and pepper. As basil purées, add oil in a slow, steady stream. With motor still running, finish with lemon juice.

Chili Pepito Pesto

Makes 2 cups

¾ cup (6 ounces) toasted
  pumpkin seeds
3 tablespoons chopped
  garlic
6 Anaheim chilies, peeled,
  seeded (see page 34 for
  directions), and roughly
  chopped
4 ounces Parmesan cheese,
  grated
Salt and freshly ground pepper to taste
½ cup olive oil

In a food processor fitted with a stainless-steel blade, finely grind pumpkin seeds and garlic. Add chilies, cheese, salt, and pepper. As chilies purée, add oil in a slow, steady stream to form a thick sauce.

Pineapple Pear Chutney

Makes 6 to 8 cups

Pineapple Pear Chutney is a tasty accompaniment to roast lamb loin, grilled rabbit, or smoked duck. It provides a sweet counterpoint and can take the place of a sauce.

1 tablespoon clarified butter
1 red onion, medium diced
5 tablespoons brandy
9 whole cloves, wrapped in
  cheesecloth
5 cinnamon sticks
½ cup red wine vinegar
1 cup apple juice
½ cup packed brown sugar
1 fresh pineapple, peeled,
  cored, and medium diced
3 fresh pears, peeled, cored,
  and medium diced
½ cup black raisins
Salt to taste

Heat butter in a large sauté pan and sauté onion until it just begins to turn translucent. Add brandy and ignite with a match, shaking pan until flames subside. Add cloves, cinnamon, vinegar, apple juice, and brown sugar and simmer for 5 minutes. Add pineapple, pears, raisins, and salt and simmer until fruit is quite tender, about 10 minutes.

Strain fruit, reserving juice, and discard clove sachet. Reduce reserved juice by half and add back to fruit. Cool and serve. May be stored in refrigerator for up to 2 weeks.

Pistou

Makes 2 cups

Pistou is a Mediterranean-influenced sauce that I like to serve warm under fish or cold under salmon mousse or Grilled Eggplant, Pepper, and Chèvre Terrine.

2 tablespoons chopped garlic
1 tablespoon chopped anchovy
1 tablespoon olive oil
6 ripe tomatoes, peeled, seeded, and roughly chopped
½ cup dry white wine
4 tablespoons chopped fresh herbs (use mint, dill, sage, fennel, lemon thyme, and basil)
Salt and freshly ground pepper to taste

Sauté garlic and anchovy in olive oil for about 1 minute. Add tomatoes and wine and simmer for about 3 minutes. Add fresh herbs and remove from heat. Season with salt and pepper.

VARIATION:

Ginger Pistou
Replace anchovy with 4 tablespoons chopped ginger. Sauté ginger with garlic and proceed.

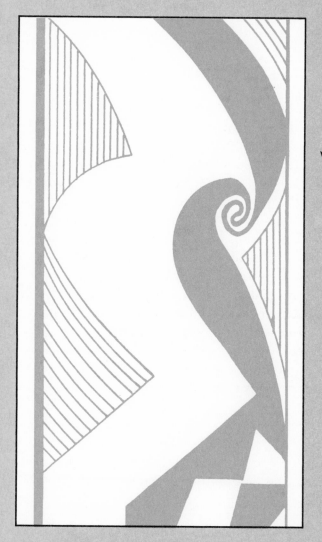

Soups

At La Réserve, Didier used to make a saffron-flavored mussel bisque that epitomized the potential for this often neglected course. The bisque was made from a rich and aromatic sabayon of eggs, cream, *jus de moules* (mussel liquid), and saffron to which were added freshly steamed mussels plucked from their shells, a fine julienne of carrot, and a tablespoon of finely chopped tomato. Didier assembled the soup in individual bowls purchased specifically for this dish. The bowls were gleaming white with a thick, two-inch-high pedestal supporting a wide-mouthed sixteen-ounce bowl which he would fill halfway up, sealing the top with puff pastry. When an order came in, the puff pastry was brushed with beaten egg and the bisque "fired" in the baking oven at 425 degrees for twenty to twenty-five minutes. As the sabayon slowly heated, it gave off steam, forcing the puff pastry to swell against its firm seal and creating a magnificent dome that baked to golden in the hot oven. The completed dish towered at least ten inches high when served. As the crusty puff pastry yielded to a customer's fork, wafts of saffron and the aroma of briny mussels escaped to perfume the air with their seductive scent.

Inspired by these statuesque bisques, I was determined that each soup at Janos would be a statement of the beauty and vitality of the cuisine. We serve two soups every night, one a hot, puff pastry soup in Didier's style and the other either a hot or cold soup depending on the season.

Saffron Mussel Bisque

Serves 4

You will need special ovenproof bowls for this bisque. The ten-ounce white ceramic bowls that I use are fairly deep and have a mouth six inches in diameter and no rim. Cut your puff pastry with a diameter one inch larger than the mouth of your bowl so that you can make a strong seal. Because the bisque needs to be completely cool before it is covered with the pastry, you should make the saffron cream several hours in advance of assembly.

Puff pastry sheets are available in many large markets.

32 fresh black mussels, cleaned and mulched
1½ cups cooking liquid from mussels
1 tablespoon chopped garlic
2 tablespoons chopped shallots
4 cups (1 quart) heavy cream
1 teaspoon saffron threads
Salt and freshly ground pepper to taste
½ cup fine julienne of carrot
½ cup skinned, seeded, and finely chopped tomato
1 egg yolk
1 tablespoon heavy cream
4 pieces puff pastry rounds

Cook mussels following the directions on page 45 but cutting recipe in half. Remove mussels from liquid and shuck; set aside. Measure out 1½ cups of the liquid for use in this recipe.

In a medium sauce pot, simmer mussel liquid with garlic and shallots until reduced by half. Add cream, stir in saffron, and season with salt and pepper. Let soup simmer until it is reduced to 3 cups. Remove from heat and refrigerate uncovered until it is completely cooled.

Preheat oven to 425°.

Divide saffron cream evenly among 4 ovenproof bowls. Divide mussels, carrot, and tomato evenly among bowls. Mix yolk and cream to make an egg wash and brush it around edges of puff pastry rounds. "Paste" a puff pastry round to the outside edge of each bowl to form a lid. Be sure pastry is firmly sealed to the bowls. Brush lids with egg wash and place bowls on bottom rack of preheated oven, allowing at least 4 inches of clearance above bowls for pastry to rise. Bake for 20 to 25 minutes. Soups are done when puff pastry rises to a well-formed and golden dome.

Wild Mushroom and Madeira Bisque

Serves 4

The Madeira cream should be made several hours in advance of assembly so that it can cool completely before being covered with the puff pastry. You will need ten-ounce ovenproof, unrimmed bowls that are fairly deep and have a wide mouth; six inches across is good. Cut the pastry rounds an inch larger in diameter than the top of the bowls.

Puff pastry sheets are available in many large markets.

3 ounces morel mushrooms
3 ounces shiitake mushrooms
4 ounces tree oyster mushrooms
Clarified butter for sautéing
1 tablespoon chopped garlic
2 tablespoons chopped shallots
4 ounces leeks, washed and cut julienne
Salt and freshly ground pepper to taste
1 cup Madeira wine
¼ cup fresh tarragon or 2 teaspoons dried tarragon
2 cups Chicken Stock (page 42)
3 cups heavy cream
1 egg yolk
1 tablespoon cream
4 pieces puff pastry rounds

Roughly chop mushrooms if they are very large; otherwise use whole. In a large sauté pan, heat enough butter to coat pan and sauté mushrooms, garlic, shallots, and leeks with salt and pepper for 2 or 3 minutes, until wilted. Add Madeira and tarragon and reduce to about ½ cup liquid so that mushrooms take on the Madeira flavor. Add stock and reduce by half. Add cream and reduce to 4 cups total. Allow to cool thoroughly before proceeding with recipe.

Preheat oven to 425°.

Divide soup evenly among 4 soup bowls. Combine yolk and cream to make an egg wash and brush it around edges of puff pastry rounds. Firmly "paste" one round of pastry to the rim of each bowl to create a lid. Brush lids with egg wash and place bowls on bottom rack of preheated oven, allowing at least 4 inches of clearance above bowls for pastry to rise. Bake for 20 to 25 minutes. Soups are done when puff pastry rises to a well-formed, golden dome.

Shrimp, Chili, and Corn Bisque

Serves 4

For this recipe you will need four 10-ounce ovenproof, unrimmed bowls, six inches in diameter at the top. You can buy puff pastry in sheets in many large markets.

16 medium-size fresh shrimp, peeled and roughly chopped

Kernels from 1 ear sweet corn

1 Anaheim chili, peeled, seeded (see page 34 for directions), and medium diced

Salt and freshly ground pepper to taste

2½ cups Lobster Sauce (page 52) at room temperature

1 egg yolk

1 tablespoon cream

4 pieces puff pastry, cut into circles with 7-inch diameters

Preheat oven to 425°.

Divide shrimp, corn, and chili evenly among bowls. Season with salt and pepper. Evenly divide Lobster Sauce among bowls. Mix yolk and cream to make an egg wash and brush it around edges of puff pastry rounds. Place pastry over each bowl, sealing brushed edges securely to bowl. Brush top of pastry well with egg wash.

Put bowls in oven, being careful to leave at least 4 inches of space above bowls for pastry to rise. Bake for about 25 minutes, until pastry is puffed and well browned. Serve immediately.

Gazpacho

Gazpacho is a hearty yet uplifting start to a meal on a hot summer day; it is also perfect as a lunch with garlic toast and a simple lettuce salad. Our version of gazpacho is from the traditional Mexican recipe that uses tomato as the base for freshly chopped vegetables. The size, shape, and uniformity of the vegetables will determine the elegance of the soup. The sizes I suggest will make a beautiful, crunchy soup. The optional garnish of sour cream and Dungeness crab meat provides a luxurious and tasty complement to a simple soup.

1 tablespoon chopped garlic

1 medium red onion, diced small

3 scallions, diced medium

1 Anaheim chili, peeled, seeded (see page 34 for directions), and diced medium

1 poblano chili, peeled, seeded, and diced small

1 cucumber, peeled, seeded, and diced medium

½ red bell pepper, diced small

½ green bell pepper, diced small

4 garden tomatoes, seeded, peeled, and diced medium

2½ cups tomato juice

¼ cup balsamic vinegar

½ cup fresh lemon juice

1 tablespoon Worcestershire sauce

Salt and freshly ground pepper to taste

4 tablespoons sour cream (optional)

4 ounces fresh, picked-over cooked Dungeness crab meat (optional)

In a large stainless-steel bowl, combine all ingredients except sour cream and crab meat. Mix well. Refrigerate for at least 12 hours, during which time the flavors in the soup will meld into a well-balanced whole.

Divide soup among 4 shallow, rimmed soup bowls. Soup may be served as is, or you can float a tablespoon of sour cream in the center of each bowl and sprinkle a couple of tablespoons of crab meat over each.

Early evening dinner service in the
porch dining room

Outside the restaurant

Salmon Carpaccio, Southwest Pepper Relish, and Two Aïolis

The Milton Duffield Room

Chilled Avocado Bisque

Serves 4

6 medium Haas avocadoes
1 teaspoon chopped garlic
1½ cups sour cream
1½ cups half-and-half
½ cup fresh lime juice
¼ teaspoon ground cumin
4 tablespoons Salsa Fresca
   (page 71) for garnish
Cilantro leaves for garnish

In a food processor fitted with a metal blade, purée avocadoes, garlic, 1¼ cups of the sour cream, half-and-half, lime juice, and cumin, working in batches. Chill for at least 1 hour. To serve, divide evenly among 4 shallow, rimmed soup bowls and float a tablespoon each of Salsa Fresca and the remaining sour cream in the center of each bowl. Decorate with cilantro leaves.

Chilled Mango Bisque

Serves 4

3 large very ripe mangos
4 limes
1 cup sour cream
1 cup milk
Strawberry Sorbet (page 214)
   for garnish
Mint leaves for garnish

Peel and seed mangos and chop roughly. Juice limes. Purée mangos with lime juice, sour cream, and milk. Chill for at least 1 hour. Serve in shallow bowls, garnishing each helping with a small scoop of sorbet and some fresh mint.

Chilled Strawberry Bisque

Serves 4

For a colorful presentation, I like to serve this soup side by side in the same bowl with Chilled Mango Bisque. Because the two soups are of similar density, it's easier to do this than you may think. Using two ladles, simply ladle the soups simultaneously into opposite sides of a shallow, flat-bottomed soup bowl.

2 pints fresh strawberries, hulled
1½ cups sour cream
¾ cup fresh lime juice
1½ cups half-and-half
Mango Sorbet (page 214) for garnish
Mint leaves for garnish

In a food processor fitted with a stainless-steel blade, completely purée all ingredients, working in batches. Chill for at least 1 hour before serving. Garnish with a small scoop of sorbet and some fresh mint.

Sherried Black Bean Soup

Serves 4

6 ounces salt pork, medium diced

1 yellow onion, medium diced

2 carrots, medium diced

3 tablespoons chopped garlic

Salt and freshly ground black pepper

1¼ cups (10 ounces) dried black beans, picked over and soaked overnight in 3 times their volume of water

3 cups Chicken Stock (page 42)

4 ounces Parmesan cheese, grated

½ cup dry sherry

1 tablespoon sour cream

1 tablespoon Cilantro Aïoli (page 66)

1 tablespoon Red Pepper Aïoli (page 66)

Sauté salt pork in a soup pot. When it begins to render fat, add onion, carrots, garlic, salt, and pepper and sauté until onion is almost translucent.

Drain and rinse beans. Add beans and stock to soup pot and simmer until beans are quite soft, about 4 hours. As soup simmers, you will have to add water to replace liquid lost to evaporation. The completed soup should be quite thick. Finish by stirring in cheese and sherry.

Divide soup among 4 soup bowls. Drizzle each serving randomly with sour cream, Cilantro Aïoli, and Red Pepper Aïoli to make a colorful abstract pattern.

Eggplant Soup

Serves 8

¼ cup olive oil
1 onion, chopped
1 carrot, chopped
4 stalks celery, chopped
4 large garlic cloves, chopped
2½ pounds eggplant, peeled and cut into 1-inch pieces
4 cups Chicken Stock (page 42)
1 cup packed fresh basil leaves
3 ounces Parmesan cheese, grated
2 cups heavy cream
½ cup medium-dry sherry
Salt and freshly ground pepper to taste
Whole basil leaves for garnish

Put oil in a stockpot. Add onion, carrot, celery, garlic, and eggplant and sauté over moderate heat for about 15 minutes or until eggplant is soft. Add stock, bring liquid to a boil, and simmer for 1 hour or until vegetables are very soft.

In a blender or food processor, purée mixture in batches with basil until smooth. Reheat the soup, stirring in cheese, cream, and sherry. Bring to a boil, season with salt and pepper, and simmer for 5 more minutes. Garnish with basil leaves and serve hot.

Appetizers

CHILES RELLENOS (STUFFED CHILIES)

*C*hiles rellenos are an important item in the Mexican food served in Sonora and southern Arizona. Typically, chilies are stuffed with mild cheese, dipped in beer batter, and fried. In Mexican restaurants they frequently appear in combination plates that also include rice, beans, and perhaps a taco or enchilada. Some recipes I've seen are casserole dishes, in which stuffed chilies are bound together with a kind of egg custard and baked.

Our interpretation gets its inspiration from the individual cheese-stuffed chilies fried in beer batter. For fillings, I like to use flavorful mixes of lobster, wild mushrooms, or sun-dried tomatoes prepared with interesting cheeses such as Brie or goat cheese. The stuffed chilies are coated with beer batter, fried, and finished in the oven. The beer batter is important both for its light, crunchy texture and for its neutral flavor, which helps temper the heat of the chili and unify the various flavors in the dish. The following beer batter can be used for all of our *relleno* recipes.

Beer Batter

Makes enough for 4 chiles rellenos

2 egg whites
1 whole egg
1 cup all-purpose flour
½ cup beer

Beat egg whites in a mixer until they form fairly stiff peaks but are not dry. In a stainless-steel bowl, lightly beat the whole egg and slowly whip in the flour, forming a batter-like consistency. Whip in beer to form a smooth liquid with no lumps. Gently fold in egg whites and refrigerate for ½ hour. Batter must be cold when using.

Lobster and Brie Chiles Rellenos

Serves 4

Phil Wood, my publisher, liked this appetizer so much the first time he ate at the restaurant that he asked me to write this cookbook just to get the recipe. I like the recipe a lot too, but now whenever I put these chilies on the menu, I think of Phil and the night he ordered three servings of them.

1 recipe Beer Batter (opposite)

4 Anaheim chilies, prepared for stuffing

8 ounces raw lobster meat, roughly chopped

2 tablespoons brandy

2 tablespoons Pernod liqueur

½ teaspoon chopped garlic

4 ounces Brie cheese

4 ounces cream cheese

Vegetable oil or clarified butter for frying

2 cups Lobster Sauce (page 52)

Salsa Fresca (page 71) for garnish

Make Beer Batter and refrigerate for ½ hour. It must be cold when you use it.

To prepare chilies for stuffing, peel them following directions on page 34. Make a slit down 1 side and remove seeds, leaving chilies otherwise intact. Set aside.

Preheat oven to 375°.

To prepare filling, combine lobster, brandy, Pernod, and garlic in a sauté pan. Ignite with a match, shaking pan until flames subside. Continue cooking until lobster is cooked through, about 3 minutes. Purée lobster and cheeses in a food processor until thoroughly blended. Using a large, plain-tipped pastry bag, pipe filling into each chili, allowing edges of slit to seal.

In a large skillet, heat enough oil or butter to coat pan. Holding chilies by the stem, individually dip them in batter, coating completely except for the stem. Place in skillet, leaving space between them, and brown well on both sides, turning once. When done, place on a cookie sheet and bake in oven for about 5 minutes, just enough to melt cheese. Meanwhile, heat Lobster Sauce and divide evenly among 4 dishes. Serve chilies on sauce, garnished with salsa.

Chiles Rellenos with Goat Cheese and Sun-Dried Tomatoes

Serves 4

1 recipe Beer Batter (page 90)
4 Anaheim chilies, prepared for stuffing
4 ounces goat cheese
4 ounces cream cheese
¼ cup (2 ounces) sun-dried tomatoes, sliced julienne
1 teaspoon chopped garlic
Vegetable oil for frying
1½ cups Roasted Garlic Sauce (page 52)
Smoked Tomato Salsa (page 72) *or* Salsa Fresca (page 71) for garnish

Make Beer Batter and refrigerate for ½ hour. It must be cold when you use it.

To prepare chilies for stuffing, peel them following directions on page 34. Make a slit down 1 side and remove seeds, leaving chilies otherwise intact. Set aside.

To make filling, blend cheeses, tomatoes, and garlic in a food processor. Using a large, plain-tipped pastry bag, pipe filling into each chili, allowing edges of slit to seal.

Holding them by the stem, dip chilies in beer batter, 1 at a time, coating completely except for the stem. Pour a thin layer of oil into a skillet, heat, and fry chilies until well browned, turning once. Heat Roasted Garlic Sauce and divide evenly among 4 dishes. Serve *chiles rellenos* on sauce, topping each with a spoonful of salsa for garnish.

Truffled Wild Mushroom Chiles Rellenos

Serves 4

The woodsy flavor of the mushrooms is heightened by the sweet heat of the chili and the rich flavor of the Madeira. This elegant refinement of a traditional preparation makes a great appetizer for a fancy dinner party. The chilies can be stuffed well in advance and the beer batter left to sit for up to 2 hours in your refrigerator, but be sure to cook the *rellenos* at the last minute or they will become soggy.

1 recipe Beer Batter (page 90)
4 Anaheim chilies, prepared for stuffing
Clarified butter for frying
6 ounces *total* morel, tree oyster, shiitake, or other wild mushrooms of your liking
½ teaspoon chopped garlic
1 tablespoon chopped truffle peelings
Salt and freshly ground pepper to taste
4 ounces Brie cheese
4 ounces cream cheese
1 cup warm Madeira Sauce (page 55)

Make Beer Batter and refrigerate for ½ hour. It must be cold when you use it.

To prepare chilies for stuffing, peel them following directions on page 34. Make a slit down 1 side and remove seeds, leaving chilies otherwise intact. Set aside.

Preheat oven to 375°.

Heat enough clarified butter in a sauté pan to coat bottom of pan. Sauté mushrooms with garlic, truffles, salt, and pepper until they begin to wilt, 2 minutes or longer depending on the mushrooms. Remove from heat and chop roughly. In a food processor, blend Brie and cream cheese, transfer them to a bowl, and fold in mushroom mixture by hand. Stuff chilies with a spoon or with a pastry bag fitted with a large plain tip.

In a nonstick sauté pan, heat more clarified butter until very hot (butter should just coat the pan). Holding chilies by the stem, immerse them in batter up to the stem and fry them 2 at a time. Brown well on all sides, then put chilies in oven for about 5 minutes to melt cheese.

Divide Madeira Sauce among 4 large warm rimmed soup bowls and place a chili in the center of each.

Roquefort, Apple, and Mango
Chiles Rellenos

Serves 4

I owe this wonderful and unusual pairing of ingredients entirely to Dora Bursey and an incredible sauternes she brought back from France one year. I wanted to make something a little off-beat but entirely complementary to the luscious, fruity wine. This dish turned out to be a great solution; the apple and Roquefort are traditional accompaniments to sauternes while the mango and chili provide a fun twist.

1 recipe Beer Batter (page 90)
4 Anaheim chilies, prepared for stuffing
4 ounces Roquefort cheese
4 ounces cream cheese
1 Granny Smith or other tart apple, peeled and finely diced
1 mango, cut into 8 thin slices
Clarified butter for frying
1 cup warm Apple Cider Sauce (page 56)

Make Beer Batter and refrigerate for ½ hour. It must be cold when you use it.

To prepare chilies for stuffing, peel them following directions on page 34. Make a slit down 1 side and remove seeds, leaving chilies otherwise intact. Set aside.

Preheat oven to 375°.

In a food processor, blend Roquefort and cream cheese and transfer them to a medium stainless-steel bowl. Fold in diced apple. Lay 2 slices of mango in each chili, then stuff chilies with cheese mixture using a pastry bag fitted with a large plain tip.

In a nonstick sauté pan, heat enough butter to coat pan until very hot. Holding chilies by the stem, immerse them in batter up to the stem and fry them 2 at a time. Brown well on all sides, then put them in oven for about 5 minutes to melt cheese.

Divide sauce among 4 large warm rimmed soup bowls and place a chili in the center of each bowl.

TAMALES

Tamales are a centuries-old component of Mexican cooking. They are made throughout Mexico, with each region having its own styles and fillings. In homes, tamale making often becomes a major family project as dozens of tamales are made at a time—plenty to eat on the spot, freeze for later, and give away to neighbors.

A typical Sonoran tamale found year-round might be filled with shredded beef stewed in a red chili sauce and wrapped in masa harina, a smooth dough made from finely milled cornmeal, shortening or lard, and water. The finished tamale is enclosed in a corn husk and steamed. In late summer and early fall, green corn harvested in the farming communities of Magdalena, Hermosillo, and cities farther south of us in Mexico provide the basis for green corn tamales. From the sweet raw kernels of green corn a masa is made that is wrapped around strips of roasted chilies and mild yellow cheese, secured in green corn husks, and steamed. A type of tamale made at Christmastime features stewed shredded beef or pork simmered with green olives and raisins in red chili sauce. Families tend to have their own special recipes for these Christmas tamales, and often give them as gifts of the season.

The tamales at Janos have been inspired by the specialties of the great home cooks around us. Although I like to work with different meats such as duck and lamb, I try to be faithful to the techniques and style of our region. The three recipes included in this book are among my favorites. They yield about two dozen tamales each, but you can easily extend them if you want to undertake more ambitious production. The following masa harina can be used for all three recipes.

Masa Harina

Makes enough for 24 tamales

4 cups masa harina (available in Mexican markets)
¾ cup Santa Cruz chili powder
1¾ cups warm water
2 tablespoons olive oil
Salt and pepper to taste

Combine masa harina and chili powder in a food processor. With motor running, slowly add water and oil and season with salt and pepper. Dough will be firm, a little elastic, and moist. It is ready to be used immediately.

Pork and Pepito Tamales

Makes 24 tamales

It is best to start this recipe a day ahead in order to give the pork butt time to cure. Then if you roast the pork on the morning of the next day, it will have time to cool before you dice it for the filling, and you will have the afternoon for the fun task of assembling the tamales.

Have some butcher's twine at hand for tying the corn husks around the tamales. You will need forty-eight pieces of six inches each.

1 cup packed brown sugar
½ cup Santa Cruz chili powder
½ cup salt
1 boneless pork butt (3½ pounds)
Vegetable oil for sautéing
2 medium yellow onions, medium diced
6 Anaheim chilies, peeled, seeded (see page 34 for directions), and medium diced
4 poblano chilies, peeled, seeded, and medium diced
3 tablespoons chopped garlic
3 tomatoes, diced
¼ cup Santa Cruz chili powder
2 tablespoons freshly ground cloves
2 tablespoons ground cinnamon
Salt and freshly ground pepper to taste
4 tablespoons tomato paste
6 ounces pepitos (pumpkin seeds), toasted

Make a cure by combining brown sugar, chili powder, and salt. Rub pork butt liberally and let cure for at least 2 hours or overnight.

Preheat oven to 350°. Without removing cure, roast pork for about 1¾ hours or until internal temperature reaches 165°. Let roast cool, then cut into a medium dice.

In a very large pan, heat a thin layer of oil. Sauté onions, chilies, and garlic for 5 minutes. Add tomatoes and season with chili powder, clove, cinnamon, salt, and pepper. Sauté for 3 minutes. Stir in diced pork and tomato paste and cook another 3 or 4 minutes before adding pepitos.

24 corn husks, soaked in
   water at least 45 minutes to
   make them pliable, then
   dried
1 recipe Masa Harina (page
   95)
1½ pounds cheddar cheese,
   grated

Prepare a steamer. Working with as many corn husks as will fit comfortably in your work space at a time, spread a thin layer of masa over the full length of each corn husk and over about three-fourths of its width. (Leaving a strip clear along one long edge will prevent the masa from doubling over onto itself when it is rolled around the filling.) Mound ¼ to ⅓ cup of filling down the length of the center of the corn husk. Spread about ¼ cup of cheese over the filling. Starting with the side opposite the clear strip, wrap masa and corn husk around filling, ending by folding the clear strip over the rolled part like a flap. Secure ends of tamale with two pieces of twine.

Steam tamales for 10 to 12 minutes or until masa is completely cooked.

Spicy Lamb Tamales

Makes 24 tamales

Have some butcher's twine at hand for securing the corn husks around the tamales. You will need forty-eight pieces, cut six inches long.

Vegetable oil for sautéing

2 pounds ground lamb (we use the trimmings from lamb saddles, but meat from the leg or shoulder is fine too)

2 large yellow onions, medium diced

6 Anaheim chilies, peeled, seeded (see page 34 for directions), and medium diced

4 poblano chilies, peeled, seeded, and medium diced

3 tablespoons chopped garlic

¼ cup Santa Cruz chili powder

2 tablespoons cumin powder

2 tablespoons freshly ground cloves

1 tablespoon chiltepin or red pepper flakes

Salt and freshly ground pepper to taste

6 ounces pine nuts, toasted

1⅔ cups raisins

½ cup fresh lime juice

24 corn husks, soaked in water at least 45 minutes to make them pliable, then dried

1 recipe Masa Harina (page 95)

1½ pounds cheddar cheese, grated

In a very large sauté pan, heat a thin layer of oil. Sauté lamb with onions, chilies, and garlic. Season mixture with chili powder, cumin, cloves, chiltepin, salt, and pepper and cook for 10 to 12 minutes, until lamb has cooked completely. Lamb tends to be fatty so don't be alarmed to find your pan half filled with grease at this point. Just pour the grease off through a strainer, pressing firmly on meat to extract all the fat.

Return meat to pan and add pine nuts, raisins, and lime juice. Cook an additional 2 or 3 minutes.

Proceed as for Pork and Pepito Tamales (page 96).

Smoked Duck and Pistachio Tamales

Makes 24 tamales

Have butcher's twine at hand for tying the corn husks around the tamales. You will need forty-eight pieces, cut six inches long.

Vegetable oil for sautéing
1 yellow onion, medium diced
2 bunches scallions, medium diced
4 Anaheim chilies, peeled, seeded (see page 34 for directions), and medium diced
2 poblano chilies, peeled, seeded, and medium diced
3 tablespoons chopped garlic
6 smoked boneless duck breasts with fat removed (see smoking chart on page 33) and medium diced
3 tablespoons Santa Cruz chili powder
Salt and freshly ground pepper to taste
½ cup fresh lime juice
6 ounces pistachios, roughly chopped
1⅔ cups golden raisins
½ cup loosely packed cilantro leaves
24 corn husks, soaked in water at least 45 minutes to make them pliable, then dried
1½ pounds cheddar cheese, grated
1 recipe Masa Harina (page 95)

In a very large pan, heat a thin layer of oil. Sauté onion, scallions, chilies, and garlic for 5 minutes. Add duck, chili powder, salt, pepper, lime juice, pistachios, and raisins and cook 5 minutes more. Stir in cilantro leaves.

Proceed as for Pork and Pepito Tamales (page 96).

Jewels of the Sea in Puff Pastry

Serves 4

A beautiful dish to present, this appetizer relies on wonderfully fresh seafood for its crisp, clean flavors. I have suggested types of seafood that I like to use. At home you can substitute whatever is freshest and most pleasing to you. Having a large variety of ingredients isn't as important as that each be impeccably fresh.

Puff pastry sheets are available in many large markets.

1 cup dry white wine
1 clove garlic, roughly chopped
8 New Zealand green lip mussels
4 crayfish
4 large Guaymas shrimp
For grilling: a mixture of ½ cup olive oil, 1 tablespoon chopped garlic, and salt and pepper to taste
4 baked puff pastry squares, cut 1½ by 1½ inches
8 large sea scallops
4 pieces salmon (1 ounce each)
1¼ cups Lobster Sauce (page 52)
2 ripe tomatoes, peeled, seeded, and chopped

Prepare a steamer using the white wine and garlic. Steam mussels just until they open. Steam crayfish; when cool enough to handle, cut shell away from tail to expose meat. Set mussels and crayfish aside.

Preheat oven to 325°. Prepare a gas or wood grill. Put a pot of water on to boil.

Brush shrimp with olive oil mixture and grill until just cooked, about 1½ minutes per side. Keep warm.

Cut puff pastry squares in half to form a top and bottom. Warm them in oven.

Simmer scallops and salmon in Lobster Sauce for 2 minutes, then add tomatoes and cook another 30 seconds.

Reheat mussels and crayfish in the boiling water or over the steamer in which you cooked them.

Place a puff pastry bottom in the center of each of 4 large warm rimmed soup bowls. Divide sauce, salmon, and scallops among the bowls and garnish with shrimp, mussels, and crayfish. Top with remaining puff pastry.

Enchanted Spring Forest in Puff Pastry

Serves 4

When I make this dish I can't help but think of spring and the rebirth it symbolizes. I picture fiddlehead ferns pushing up through the moist, verdant undergrowth of a rejuvenating forest or morels growing from the very decay that provides the life of the forest. It's exciting for me to get these products; even their arrival sets me to imagining myself in the forest exploring the beauty of spring as I discover these treasures of nature.

Puff pastry sheets are available in many large markets.

12 stalks tender, thin
    asparagus
4 baked puff pastry squares,
    cut 1½ by 1½ inches
1 tablespoon chopped garlic
8 ounces morels, rinsed,
    picked over, and dried
6 ounces fiddlehead ferns
1¼ cups Madeira Sauce
    (page 55)
2 ripe tomatoes, peeled,
    seeded, and chopped
Salt and freshly ground pepper to taste
8 nasturtium, borage,
    Johnny-jump-ups, or other
    edible blossoms for garnish

Preheat oven to 325°.

Trim and cook asparagus in boiling, lightly salted water for 3 to 4 minutes until just tender. Remove asparagus to a bowl of ice water to stop the cooking; reserve hot water for reheating asparagus later.

Cut puff pastry squares in half to form tops and bottoms and warm them in oven.

Simmer garlic, morels, and fiddlehead ferns in Madeira Sauce for 2 to 3 minutes, then add tomato and simmer an additional 45 seconds. Season with salt and pepper.

To assemble, reheat asparagus in reserved hot water. Place a puff pastry bottom in the center of each of 4 large warm rimmed soup bowls. Divide sauce, morels, ferns, and tomatoes over the puff pastry. Compose asparagus in the bowls and top with remaining puff pastry. Garnish each portion with two blossoms.

Grand-Mère Petreau's Mussel and Artichoke Pithiviers

Serves 6 as an appetizer and 2 as a main course

Didier showed me this dish one afternoon at La Réserve. As he was attaching and shaping the puff pastry top he said, "I could make this perfectly round if I wanted to, but this is my grandmother's dish and hers was always a little rough and irregular, so I make mine that way too." What a dish Didier's *grand-mère* had made, with layers of sliced artichoke bottom, mussels removed from their shells, and tomatoes all baked together in a double-crust puff pastry tart.

The name *pithiviers* refers to the town in France where this kind of tart originated. I always cut the pithiviers into thirds and serve one slice with Beurre Blanc sauce as an appetizer, but a whole pithiviers would make a generous individual main course.

Puff pastry sheets are available in many large markets.

4 puff pastry rounds (2 with 6-inch diameters and 2 with 7-inch diameters)
Flour for flouring work surface
3 large artichokes, trimmed to leave just the bottoms and cooked in water with lemon juice, peppercorns, and bay leaves until tender (about 30 minutes), then chilled and thinly sliced
4 tomatoes, peeled, seeded, and chopped
Salt and freshly ground pepper to taste
24 mussels, steamed and removed from their shells
Egg wash made from 1 beaten egg and 1 tablespoon milk
1 cup warm Beurre Blanc sauce (page 58)

Preheat oven to 425°.

Use the 6-inch pastry round for the bottom of the tarts. Lay bottoms on a lightly floured work table. Leaving a ¼-inch rim all around, lay slices of artichoke in concentric circles on each bottom. Cover artichoke with a layer of tomato sprinkled with salt and pepper, and then top tomato with mussels.

Cut a ½-inch steam hole in the center of each 7-inch pastry round. Brush "rims" of bottom rounds with some of the egg wash and place larger rounds on top, sealing rims well by crimping them with the tines of a fork. Brush tops with remaining egg wash and place tarts on a cookie sheet. Bake until they have completely risen and are well browned, about 30 minutes.

Serve whole or sliced with Beurre Blanc sauce.

Smoked Salmon, Leek, and Brie Pithiviers

Serves 6 as an appetizer and 2 as a main course

Puff pastry sheets are available in many large markets.

4 puff pastry rounds (2 with 6-inch diameters and 2 with 7-inch diameters)

Flour for flouring work surface

3 tablespoons Pommeray or other whole-grain mustard

10 ounces Brie cheese, cut into 10 thin slices

2 leeks, washed, sliced julienne (you should have about 2 cups), and sautéed with 1 teaspoon chopped garlic and salt and pepper to taste for about 3 minutes, until quite soft

8 ounces smoked salmon chunks (preferably hickory-smoked)

Egg wash made from 1 beaten egg and 1 tablespoon milk

1 cup warm Dill Beurre Blanc sauce (page 58)

Preheat oven to 425°.

Use the 6-inch pastry round for the bottoms of the tarts. Lay bottoms on a lightly floured work table. Leaving a ¼-inch rim all around, lightly brush each bottom with mustard. Lay Brie over bottoms, leaving rims free. Cover Brie with leeks, then with salmon.

Cut a ½-inch steam hole in the center of each 7-inch pastry round. Brush rims of bottom rounds with some of the egg wash and place tops on each, sealing edges well by crimping them with the tines of a fork. Brush tops with remaining egg wash and place tarts on a cookie sheet. Bake until they have completely risen and are well browned, about 30 minutes.

Serve whole or sliced with Dill Beurre Blanc sauce.

Asparagus Mousseline in Puff Pastry

Serves 4

Puff pastry sheets are available in many large markets.

4 bunches asparagus
  (4 ounces each), trimmed
  and bundled
4 puff pastry rectangles (2 by
  4 inches)
2 cups Mousseline Sauce
  (page 65)
½ red bell pepper, finely
  diced, for garnish

Preheat oven to 450°.

Cook asparagus in lightly salted water until al dente (about 3 minutes), then shock by immediately submerging in ice water to stop cooking. Drain. Keep cooking water hot for reheating asparagus later.

Place puff pastry in oven and bake until completely risen and well browned, about 12 minutes. Cut each pastry shell in half, placing top halves in turned-off oven to keep them warm and bottom halves on sides of individual serving plates.

Rewarm asparagus briefly in reserved water, drain again, and place one bunch on top of each rectangle, with tips arranged in fan away from pastry. Cover pastry and tips of asparagus with foil, and spoon Mousseline Sauce in a ribbon across exposed part of asparagus. Gratinée by placing directly under broiler and browning well.

Remove foil and place top half back on puff pastry. Sprinkle with red bell pepper and serve immediately.

PASTA

Pasta dishes have long been a staple on our menus. The noodles themselves are relatively easy to make with a small rolling machine. There are scores of recipes for pasta dough, each varying slightly in the proportions of ingredients and in the substances used to color or flavor the noodles. In one of its simplest forms, pasta dough is made with all-purpose flour, water, eggs, and a little oil. More complex doughs may be flavored with anything from cracked pepper to spinach to squid ink. No matter what the recipe, the proportions will vary with the humidity, the moisture content of the flour, the size of the eggs, and the moisture content of the flavoring agent. Consider the recipes in this book a point of departure as you determine what is suitable for your conditions and ingredients.

Different shapes of noodles can be made from the same recipe, depending on how they are cut. Fettuccine is thin, flat, and about ¼ inch wide; linguini is thin, flat, and quite narrow; spaghetti is thin and round; ravioli are small "packets" that are stuffed with various fillings. The Italians have created dozens of different shapes for noodles, many of which are interchangeable in recipes and some of which are specific to certain recipes. The shapes and flavors of pasta that I have selected for this book provide a good introduction to different techniques.

All of my recipes call for a pasta rolling machine. For centuries, though, pasta was rolled by hand with a rolling pin, flour, and elbow grease and cut with a knife. Don't let the lack of a machine keep you from enjoying homemade pasta.

Basic Food Processor Pasta

Serves 6 to 8, depending on use

1 to 1½ cups unbleached all-
   purpose flour
1 to 1½ cups semolina flour
Salt to taste
3 large eggs, lightly beaten
2 tablespoons olive oil

Place flours and salt in a food processor fitted with a stainless-steel blade and pulse motor to mix. With motor running, add eggs and process until dough resembles coarse meal, about 20 seconds. Add oil and process until dough forms a ball, another 10 to 15 seconds. Remove dough, cut into three portions, and cover with a slightly damp cloth to prevent drying. Let dough rest for 10 minutes.

To roll dough, set up rolling machine. Set up wooden dowels between chairs for drying. Using a third of the recipe at a time, flatten dough by hand so that it will fit through widest setting of machine. Dust dough lightly with flour to prevent sticking. Run dough through widest setting, then fold over onto itself and repeat through widest setting until dough is smooth and somewhat elastic.

Lightly dust dough again and run it through machine at the next thinnest setting. Repeat this procedure with each setting, continuing to dust with flour until you've reached the thickness you desire. Cut dough sheet down to a workable size if it becomes too long to manage easily.

As each sheet is finished, lay it over dowels to dry. The length of time the noodles should dry before cutting depends on the heat and humidity of your kitchen and the moisture of the dough. The dough should be partially dry but not stiff or brittle or it will crack when cut. If it is too moist it will stick in the machine. Pasta used for canneloni and ravioli should not be dried.

Select cutter attachment appropriate to your recipe and feed dough sheet through blades. Cut pasta can be cooked immediately or dried completely and stored.

Cook noodles in a large pot of boiling, well-salted water with about 2 teaspoons of olive oil per quart of water. Fresh pasta cooks quickly, in 30 to 45 seconds if quite thin and in slightly more time if thick. Check for doneness by biting a strand and looking at its cross section. If dough is cooked through, it is done. Do not overcook.

Strain pasta in a colander and rinse with cold water. Toss with enough olive oil to prevent sticking. For additional flavor, pasta can also be tossed with salt, pepper, and garlic. Use pasta in your selected recipe.

Green Chili Pasta

Serves 6 to 8, depending on use

This pasta is great cut into fettuccine and tossed with Roasted Garlic Sauce that has been simmered with diced chilies, scallions, shrimp, and tomatoes.

2 Anaheim chilies, peeled, seeded (see page 34 for directions), and roughly chopped
2 poblano chilies, peeled, seeded, and roughly chopped
1 recipe Basic Food Processor Pasta (opposite), with flour increased by about ¾ cup

Purée chilies until they are smooth. Force purée through a strainer to remove any lumps. Proceed as for basic pasta recipe, adding purée with oil and blending well. (This pasta will take longer to dry.)

Beet Pasta

Serves 6 to 8, depending on use

This recipe makes a gorgeous, burgundy-color noodle. Cut into fettuccine, Beet Pasta is pretty and tasty when simmered with white wine, goat
cheese, sun-dried tomatoes, and a bit of cream, then tossed with cilantro
leaves and sprinkled with ground pistachio nuts.

2 large beets, peeled
Salt to taste
1 recipe Basic Food Processor Pasta (page 106), with
flour increased by about
¾ cup

Boil beets in salted water for about 1 hour, until
they are quite tender. Place in a food processor and purée
until smooth. Force purée through a strainer to remove
any lumps. Proceed as for basic pasta recipe, adding purée
with oil and blending well. (This pasta will take longer to
dry.)

Squid Ink Pasta

Serves 6 to 8, depending on use

Squid ink must be laboriously collected from the sacks of squid, making
the ink relatively expensive but worth it for the beautiful black pasta that
can be made from it. The ink is available in specialty stores in one ounce
packets of powder or liquid. One packet produces a very dark pasta.
Squid ink does not have much flavor in this concentration but no matter,
since it is used mostly for its color.

I like to cut Squid Ink Pasta into linguini and simmer it with Pistou and bay scallops, then sprinkle it with grated Parmesan cheese. The
dish is a tasty and beautiful first course or entrée.

1 packet squid ink
1 recipe Basic Food Processor Pasta (page 106)

Proceed as for basic pasta recipe, adding squid ink
with eggs and processing a bit longer if necessary to completely incorporate ink.

Flower of Cilantro Pasta

Serves 6 to 8, depending on use

In this technique, the pasta is not colored but rather "imprinted" with leaves of cilantro that are rolled into it during the final pass through the roller. This stretches and presses the leaves, imbedding them in the dough sheets much like flowers pressed between wax paper. The flower-embossed pasta can be used either for a very special lasagna or as a garnish, as in Seafood Stew in Flower of Cilantro Blanket.

⅓ recipe Basic Food Processor Pasta (page 106)

6 to 8 perfect cilantro leaves, with stems completely removed

Roll pasta to final setting on your roller. Cut six to eight 4-inch squares from the pasta, reserving rest for another purpose. Place a cilantro leaf in half of each square and fold flap over top so that leaf is sandwiched in the center of the folded square.

Run each piece through roller, folded side first, until desired thickness is reached. Be careful that cilantro doesn't slip out during rolling.

Lightly flour pasta squares and reserve to be cooked to order. It is best to cook them within an hour of making them, but if you can't, rub them with a little oil and store them in the refrigerator. They will keep this way for up to 2 days.

Chili Linguini with Madeira Crème Fraîche and Truffles

Serves 6 to 8

A New Year's Eve with truffles on the menu provides even more to celebrate. In this recipe truffles are sprinkled over chili linguini, which is itself curled in a heap on a rich pool of Madeira reduced in crème fraîche.

3 cups Madeira wine
2 tablespoons chopped garlic
2 tablespoons chopped shallots
1½ cups crème fraîche
Salt and freshly ground pepper to taste
1 recipe Green Chili Pasta (page 107), cut into linguini
2 to 3 large black truffles (if using canned, save juice)

In a large sauté pan, bring Madeira, garlic, and shallots to a boil and reduce to 1 cup liquid. This will take about 20 minutes. Add truffle juice, if any, and whisk in crème fraîche and season with salt and pepper.

Cook pasta.

Divide sauce among 4 large warm rimmed soup bowls. Curl linguini around a fork and place it in equal mounds in each bowl. Garnish by grating truffles over each mound.

Lobster Ravioli Tic-Tac-Toe with Three Caviars

Serves 6

These ravioli are another New Year's Eve appetizer. The three caviars arranged in a diagonal tic-tac-toe to victory make a festive garnish, and the ravioli themselves are delicious.

LOBSTER FILLING
Olive oil for sautéing
¾ pound uncooked lobster tail meat, medium diced
¼ pound domestic mushrooms, medium diced
2 bunches scallions, medium diced
3 tablespoons chopped garlic
3 tablespoons brandy
1 tablespoon Pernod liqueur
1 tablespoon Pommeray or other whole-grain mustard
½ cup grated Parmesan cheese
Salt and freshly ground pepper to taste

RAVIOLI PASTA
1 recipe Basic Food Processor Pasta (page 106)
Flour for flouring work surface
Egg wash made from 1 egg whipped with 1 tablespoon milk

To make filling, heat a thin layer of oil in a large sauté pan and sauté lobster, mushrooms, scallions, and garlic for 2 minutes over high heat. Pour in brandy and Pernod and ignite with a match. Shake pan until flames subside, then stir in mustard, cheese, salt, and pepper and cook for 2 minutes more or until lobster is cooked through. Set aside.

To make ravioli, roll pasta into 8 strips, 5 inches wide and 14 inches long. Pasta should be quite thin but still workable. Keeping reserves moist under a slightly dampened cloth, work with 1 strip at a time on a lightly floured work surface. Evenly space 6 tight mounds of lobster filling (1½ teaspoons each) over the pasta sheet. Brush egg wash around the mounds, then lay a second sheet on top, molding the pasta around each mound, pushing out any pockets, and forming a tight seal. Using a fluted ravioli cutter, cut each ravioli in a circle or square. Cook ravioli in 1 gallon boiling salted water for 2 or 3 minutes, until sealed edges are cooked through.

CONTINUED →

TIC-TAC-TOE

1½ cups warm Lobster
   Sauce (page 52)
24 lengths of chive, cut
   6 inches long
3 ounces beluga or sevruga
   caviar
3 ounces American golden
   caviar
3 ounces flying fish caviar

To assemble dish, divide sauce among 6 warm large rimmed soup bowls. Arrange 4 ravioli in an open square in the sauce and place 4 chives in a tic-tac-toe figure over them. Put ½ ounce of each caviar in 3 squares so that the 3 caviars form a winning diagonal.

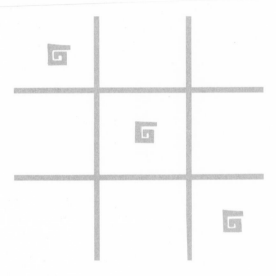

Seafood Stew in Flower of Cilantro Blanket

Serves 4

12 New Zealand green lip mussels, scrubbed and bearded (black mussels may be substituted)
4 cups (1 quart) dry white wine
4 tablespoons chopped garlic
8 crayfish, steamed, *or* 8 large shrimp, peeled and deveined
2 Anaheim chilies, peeled, seeded (see page 34 for directions), and medium diced
1 bunch scallions, sliced to ½-inch lengths
2 tomatoes, peeled, seeded, and medium diced
12 sea scallops
For grilling: a mixture of ½ cup olive oil, 1 tablespoon chopped garlic, and salt and pepper to taste
4 squares Flower of Cilantro Pasta (page 109)
¾ cup picked-over, loosely packed cilantro leaves

Prepare a gas or wood grill. Put a pot of water on to boil.

Steam mussels over wine and garlic until they open (4 to 6 minutes for green lip mussels, 2 to 3 minutes for black mussels). Remove mussels. Steam crayfish; remove and, when cool, cut shell from around tail so that tail meat is exposed. Reduce steaming liquid to 2 cups. Add chilies, scallions, and tomatoes and cook an additional 2 minutes. Set mussel liquid aside.

Brush scallops and shrimp, if used, with olive oil mixture. Grill scallops for about 1 minute per side and shrimp for 2 to 3 minutes per side. Keep warm while assembling dish.

Cook pasta squares in lightly salted boiling water until cooked through, about 30 seconds. Remove and sprinkle with olive oil so that they don't stick to each other. Reserve water for reheating pasta.

Reheat mussels and crayfish in mussel liquid, and pasta in the reserved water. Divide mussel liquid among 4 warm large rimmed soup bowls and arrange scallops in the middle of the bowls with crayfish and mussels on the outside. Sprinkle bowls with cilantro leaves and drape a sheet of pasta over the center of each bowl.

Warm Sea and Forest Nasturtium Salad

Serves 6 as an appetizer and 4 as a main course

To give this recipe its unique blend of flavors, the shrimp, mushrooms, and asparagus must be grilled on a barbecue, preferably over mesquite or hickory wood.

CHILI VINAIGRETTE

1 egg yolk
1 tablespoon Santa Cruz chili powder
1 teaspoon finely chopped garlic
¾ cup olive oil
¼ cup fresh lime juice
Salt and freshly ground pepper to taste

SHRIMP AND VEGETABLES

20 large Guaymas shrimp, peeled and deveined
1 pound tree oyster mushrooms
1 pound asparagus, blanched and chilled, *or* ½ pound snow peas, blanched and chilled
For grilling: a mixture of ½ cup olive oil, 1 tablespoon chopped garlic, and salt and pepper to taste

Assorted baby lettuces, washed and well dried (for a main course, use a large handful for each person; for an appetizer, use the same total amount divided among 6 plates)
36 nasturtium flowers

In a medium-size stainless-steel bowl, prepare vinaigrette by whisking together egg yolk, chili powder, and garlic. Whisk in olive oil in a slow, steady stream. Season with salt and pepper.

Using wood such as mesquite or hickory to enhance flavor, heat barbecue until coals are ashen. Dip shrimp in olive oil mixture to coat lightly and place on grill, allowing about 3 minutes for each side. Shrimp is done when it turns pinkish-orange. Do not overcook or shrimp will be dry.

When shrimp is half cooked, toss mushrooms in olive oil mixture to coat lightly, place on grill, and cook for 3 minutes, turning constantly. (As these mushrooms have a high moisture content and cook very quickly, take care not to overcook them.)

When shrimp and mushrooms are nearly finished, toss asparagus or snow peas in olive oil mixture to coat lightly and heat on grill, about 1 minute.

To assemble, toss lettuces in half of dressing and arrange on individual plates. Toss warm mushrooms, shrimp, and 20 nasturtium flowers in remaining dressing and arrange on top of lettuces. Garnish with asparagus or snow peas and with remaining flowers.

Shrimp and Chili Paupiettes with Nectarine Relish and Avocado

Serves 4

The French name of this dish refers to wrapping the chili around a grilled shrimp. The presentation is dramatic, the flavors fresh and cooling.

AVOCADO SAUCE

1 medium to large Haas avocado
½ cup sour cream
Juice of 2 limes
Salt and freshly ground pepper to taste

NECTARINE RELISH

2 large nectarines, peeled and diced small
¼ cup finely diced red onion
1 teaspoon seeded and very finely diced jalapeño chili
2 tablespoons fresh orange juice
12 orange sections, with membranes removed
¼ cup loosely packed mint leaves, cut into a fine chiffonade

SHRIMP AND CHILIES

12 large shrimp, peeled and deveined, with tails left on
For grilling: a mixture of ½ cup olive oil, 1 tablespoon chopped garlic, and salt and pepper to taste
3 Anaheim chilies, peeled, seeded (see page 34 for directions), and cut into ½-inch by ½-inch strips

12 small Belgian endive leaves for garnish

Prepare a gas or wood grill.

To make sauce, purée avocado, sour cream, and lime juice in a food processor and strain through a fine strainer. Season with salt and pepper. Set aside in refrigerator.

To make relish, combine nectarines, onion, chili, and orange juice in a bowl. Toss lightly. Fold in orange sections and mint chiffonade. Set aside in refrigerator.

Brush shrimp with olive oil mixture and grill until just cooked through, 2 to 3 minutes per side. Place chili strips briefly on grill in order to warm them.

To assemble, wrap a chili-strip band around the middle of each shrimp. Divide sauce among 4 chilled plates. Mound relish toward the edge of each plate and garnish with 3 Belgian endive "feathers" radiating from the relish over the rim of the plate. Arrange 3 shrimp radiating spoke-like from the other side of the relish.

Grilled Eggplant, Pepper, and Chèvre Terrine

Serves 8 to 12

This cold vegetarian terrine is ideal as an appetizer served with Pistou and garlic toast, as part of an antipasto platter, or as an item in your picnic basket.

You will need some special equipment for this recipe: a loaf pan 9¼ by 5¼ by 2¾ inches; plastic wrap for lining the mold; cardboard cut to sit snugly on top of the mold; and two bricks for weighting down the terrine.

2 medium-size eggplants, peeled and cut into ½-inch-thick rounds (reserve any odd-size pieces)

For grilling: a mixture of 1 cup olive oil, 2 tablespoons chopped garlic, and salt and pepper to taste

3 Anaheim chilies, peeled, seeded (see page 34 for directions), and flattened out

3 green bell peppers, peeled, seeded (see page 34 for directions), and flattened out

3 red bell peppers, peeled, seeded, and flattened out

8 ounces goat cheese, crumbled

Prepare a wood or gas grill. Brush eggplant with olive oil mixture and grill until soft throughout, 3 to 5 minutes per side. Let eggplant cool.

Line loaf pan with plastic wrap and layer terrine in this order:

- Eggplant rounds, supplemented by additional pieces to form a solid base (will be top when unmolded)
- Red peppers
- Goat cheese
- Eggplant
- Chilies
- Goat cheese
- Green peppers
- Eggplant

Cover top with plastic wrap, add cardboard cut to fit terrine, and place bricks on top of cardboard. Refrigerate for at least 24 hours before unmolding.

Desert landscape

Asparagus Mousseline in Puff Pastry

Picking up mangos with Harvey Bracker and my son Ben

My father-in-law, Harvey Bracker, getting mangos from Lucas Barreda at Sunbelt Fruit and Vegetables in Nogales

Janos Antipasto Platter

Serves 6 as an appetizer, 4 as a main course, and 6 to 14 as a party platter

We serve a variety of antipasto platters, which are essentially a sampling of cold salads and condiments. This assortment is one of my favorites and can be served as an appetizer, a main course, or a party platter.

4 to 6 portions Grilled Eggplant, Pepper, and Chèvre Terrine (opposite), sliced ½ inch to ¾ inch thick

12 slices ripe, plump garden tomatoes

8 yellow plum tomatoes, cut in half lengthwise

2 to 4 Haas avocadoes (may be more or less depending on size of avocadoes and number of guests)

12 to 24 Greek olives

2 or 3 baby artichokes, steamed, grilled, cooled, and cut in half

3 tablespoons Garlic Aïoli (page 66)

3 tablespoons Opal Basil Vinaigrette (page 67)

Attractively arrange vegetables on as many plates as necessary. Put a small dollop of aïoli on the cut side of each artichoke. Drizzle tomatoes and avocadoes with vinaigrette.

Salmon Carpaccio with Southwest Pepper Relish and Two Aïolis

Serves 4

In this recipe we've taken the carpaccio technique—which calls for a slice of beef tenderloin pounded paper-thin to be served raw with olive oil and Roquefort for garnish—and applied it to salmon. We use absolutely fresh salmon, slice it thinly, and pound it to translucence with virgin olive oil. Composed on the plate with the salmon is a petite salad of baby lettuces, and the salmon itself is garnished with drizzles of red and green aïolis and a sprinkling of a colorful pepper relish. This dish makes a pretty, cool, and luscious appetizer in the summer when king salmon is plentiful. Our customers enjoy the playful interpretation of a classic recipe and find it a nonthreatening preparation of raw fish.

SOUTHWEST PEPPER RELISH

1 tablespoon very finely diced red bell pepper
1 tablespoon very finely diced yellow bell pepper
1 tablespoon peeled, seeded (page 34), and very finely diced Anaheim chili
½ teaspoon fresh lemon juice
¼ teaspoon virgin olive oil
⅛ teaspoon very finely chopped garlic
Salt and freshly ground pepper to taste

SALMON AND LETTUCE GARNISH

4 pieces thinly sliced, very fresh king or Norwegian salmon (1½ ounces each)
1 teaspoon virgin olive oil
Salt and freshly ground pepper to taste
Enough lettuce for 4 small servings (I like a mix of curly endive, oak leaf, Belgian endive, and radicchio)
¼ cup Walnut Vinaigrette (page 68) for coating lettuce leaves
2 tablespoons Cilantro Aïoli (page 66)
2 tablespoons Red Pepper Aïoli (page 66)

To prepare relish, combine all ingredients and mix well. Set aside.

To prepare carpaccio, sprinkle each piece of salmon with olive oil, salt, and pepper. Sandwich each between 12- by 12-inch sheets of plastic wrap. Gently pound salmon with the flat edge of a heavy French knife, slowly flattening it until it is a thin, virtually translucent sheet.

Peel off plastic wrap and lay salmon on 4 medium-size appetizer plates. Toss lettuces in vinaigrette and arrange small salads to the side of salmon. Using small pastry bags fitted with fine tips, drizzle aïolis in a crisscross pattern over carpaccio, then sprinkle carpaccio with relish.

Ahi Carpaccio with Sesame Aïoli and Grilled Shiitake Mushrooms; Pickled Ginger

Serves 4

This dish is really a synthesis of sushi garnishes and carpaccio presentation. Pickled ginger provides a fiery accent to the sweet, succulent Hawaiian tuna and the grilled mushrooms, while the mild, pleasing taste of the aïoli unifies the dish. You can easily make pickled ginger at home, or you can purchase it in Asian specialty stores.

4 thin, skinless slices very fresh ahi (1½ ounces each)
1 teaspoon virgin olive oil
Salt and freshly ground pepper to taste
8 large shiitake mushrooms
For grilling: a mixture of ½ cup olive oil, 1 tablespoon chopped garlic, and salt and pepper to taste
2 tablespoons Pickled Ginger (recipe follows)
2 tablespoons Sesame Aïoli (use Mayonnaise, page 66, made without mustard and using sesame oil instead of olive oil, and with 1 teaspoon toasted sesame seeds folded in at the end)

Sprinkle each piece of ahi with olive oil, salt, and pepper and sandwich it between 12- by 12-inch sheets of plastic wrap. Gently pound ahi with the flat edge of a heavy French knife, slowly flattening it until it is a thin, virtually translucent sheet. Set aside.

Prepare a gas or wood grill. Brush mushrooms with olive oil mixture and grill them for about 1 minute per side. Let them cool.

Peel plastic wrap off ahi and lay 1 piece flat in the center of each of 4 medium-sized appetizer plates. In the center of each carpaccio, form a rosette from Pickled Ginger. Put 2 mushrooms next to each rosette. Place aïoli in a small pastry bag fitted with a fine tip, and drizzle decoratively over carpaccio.

Pickled Ginger

Makes 1 cup

2 ginger roots, peeled and sliced very thinly
Rice wine vinegar to cover
3 tablespoons granulated sugar

Combine all ingredients and allow to marinate for at least 4 hours before using. Can be stored in glass in the refrigerator for up to a week.

Grilled Tilapia Paillard with Sauté of Bay Scallops and Wild Mushrooms

Serves 4

This is one of my favorite preparations for the sweet, firm fish that is raised west of us in Gila Bend. Tilapia fillets are naturally quite thin and lend themselves perfectly to this cooking technique. A latticework of roasted chilies is a fun garnish.

Clarified butter for sautéing
4 ounces bay scallops
4 ounces tree oyster mushrooms
4 scallions, sliced in ½-inch lengths
½ tablespoon chopped garlic
Salt and freshly ground black pepper
2 tablespoons brandy
4 skinless fillets tilapia (3 ounces each)
For grilling: a mixture of ½ cup olive oil, 1 tablespoon chopped garlic, and salt and pepper to taste
2 Anaheim chilies, peeled, seeded (see page 34 for directions), and cut into 16 narrow strips 4 inches long

Prepare a gas or wood grill.

In a small sauté pan, heat enough clarified butter to coat pan. Sauté scallops, mushrooms, and scallions with garlic, salt, and pepper for about 1 minute. Add brandy and ignite with a match, shaking pan vigorously until flames subside. Cook 1 more minute to finish cooking scallops. Set aside but keep warm.

Brush tilapia lightly with olive oil mixture and grill for about 2 minutes per side on the hottest part of the grill. Warm chili strips on grill.

Place tilapia in the middle of 4 warm appetizer plates and arrange chilies in a crisscross pattern on top of fish. Serve wild mushroom sauté as a garnish mounded next to each fillet.

Grilled Salmon Paillard with Lobster Beurre Blanc

Serves 4

Paillard refers to a cut of meat, poultry, or fish that is thinly sliced and cooked very quickly over high heat to sear the outside and seal in flavor. For this dish we grill thin slices of king or Norwegian salmon. Care must be taken when grilling the salmon because the slices will cook in about 30 seconds, so you must work quickly and have everything ready to go in advance. Overcooked salmon becomes dry and somewhat tasteless instead of being moist and sweet.

6 ounces bay scallops
1 pound king or Norwegian salmon, cut into 12 thin fillets
Salt and freshly ground pepper to taste
For grilling: a mixture of ½ cup olive oil, 1 tablespoon chopped garlic, and salt and pepper to taste
¾ cup warm Lobster Beurre Blanc sauce (page 58)

Prepare a gas or wood grill.

Sprinkle scallops and salmon with salt and pepper and brush scallops with olive oil mixture. Grill scallops for 2 minutes and hold warm. (If the grates on your grill are too wide, you may sauté scallops in a little olive oil.) Lightly brush salmon with olive oil mixture and grill for 15 to 20 seconds per side.

Divide sauce among 4 warm appetizer plates and on each plate arrange 3 slices of salmon. Sprinkle each helping with scallops.

Broiled Oysters with Red Pepper Pesto; Spicy Lamb Sausage

Serves 4

We frequently serve oysters in the winter. This recipe pairing oysters and a spicy lamb sausage is one of my favorites. It's an unusual but satisfying flavor combination and is hearty enough to be a filling starter on a cool January evening.

RED PEPPER PESTO

4 red bell peppers, cut into chunks
¼ tablespoon chopped garlic
½ cup finely chopped blanched almonds
4 ounces Parmesan cheese, grated
¾ cup olive oil
Salt and freshly ground pepper to taste

OYSTERS AND LAMB SAUSAGE

12 fresh prime oysters on the half shell (use your favorite variety, as long as they are very fresh)
8 patties grilled Spicy Lamb Sausage (recipe follows)
6 tablespoons Salsa Fresca (page 71)
2 cups rock salt for presentation

To prepare pesto, purée red pepper in a food processor. With motor running, add garlic, almonds, and cheese and process until fully combined. With motor still running, add oil in a slow, steady stream so that it is completely incorporated. Season with salt and pepper.

Preheat an overhead broiler. Top each oyster with 1 tablespoon pesto and broil for 1 to 1½ minutes, just until pesto begins to brown.

Spread rock salt over *half* the surface of 4 dinner plates and nestle 3 oysters in the salt on each plate. (The salt holds the heat and also keeps the oysters from sliding.)

Place 2 sausage patties on each of 4 smaller plates and garnish with salsa. Put sausage plates on clear half of dinner plates.

CONTINUED →

Spicy Lamb Sausage

Makes 1 pound

1 pound fresh lamb, ground medium coarse (we use the trimming from lamb saddles, but lamb shoulder would also be fine)

4 tablespoons fresh lime juice

2 teaspoons chiltepin or red pepper flakes

4 tablespoons chopped garlic

¾ cup lightly packed cilantro leaves

Salt and freshly ground pepper to taste

Prepare a gas or wood grill, or preheat an overhead broiler. Thoroughly combine all ingredients by hand and form into 8 patties of about 2 ounces each. Grill or broil patties and hold warm for serving with oysters.

Blue Corn Fritters

Serves 6 to 8

1 recipe Beer Batter (page 90)

4 cups blue cornmeal

3 cups water

1 tablespoon chopped cilantro

¼ cup finely diced red bell pepper

½ cup finely diced red onion

Kernels from 1 ear sweet corn

1 Anaheim chili, peeled, seeded (see page 34 for directions), and finely diced

½ tablespoon chopped garlic

Clarified butter for frying

Make Beer Batter and refrigerate for ½ hour. It must be cold when you use it.

Blend cornmeal and water until mixture has a moist consistency. Combine cilantro, pepper, onion, corn, chili, and garlic and add to cornmeal. Mix well.

To make fritters, fold cornmeal mixture into an equal amount of Beer Batter. In an 8-inch nonstick pan, heat enough butter to coat bottom of pan. Drop in cornmeal mixture in 2-tablespoon dollops, frying and turning until brown on both sides. Do not crowd pan, and add more butter as needed. Serve 2 fritters per person.

Trilogy of Blue Corn Fritters

Serves 4

A frequent appetizer on our Menu of the Evening, this lively dish combines many different flavors. It features three of our salsas that rated as "Best in Tucson" at a Mexican food cook-off. The salsas are served on Blue Corn Fritters and are individually topped with grilled shrimp, lobster, and salmon. At home, you may choose to simplify things by using only one salsa and one type of seafood. The dish will still be enjoyable, just not as exciting.

4 salmon fillets (1½ ounces each)

4 chunks raw lobster tail (1½ ounces each)

4 large Guaymas shrimp, unpeeled

For grilling: a mixture of ½ cup olive oil, 1 tablespoon chopped garlic, and salt and pepper to taste

2 Blue Corn Fritters, each 8 inches in diameter (use half of recipe on page 124)

¾ cup warm Lobster Sauce (page 52)

4 tablespoons Tomatillo Salsa (page 71)

4 tablespoons Salsa Fresca (page 71)

4 tablespoons Smoked Tomato Salsa (page 72)

Prepare a gas or wood grill. Brush seafood with olive oil mixture and grill. Cook salmon for about 2 minutes total and lobster and shrimp for about 3 minutes total. Turn once.

Cut each fritter into 6 wedges. Divide sauce among 4 appetizer plates and arrange 3 fritter triangles on each plate. On each triangle on a plate, put a different kind of salsa. Place shrimp on Tomatillo Salsa, lobster on Salsa Fresca, and salmon on Smoked Tomato Salsa.

Wild Mushroom and Smoked Poblano Flan

Serves 6

We serve this flan with Salsa Fresca and Black Beans.

2 poblano chilies
2 Anaheim chilies
12 ounces tree oyster
    mushrooms
For grilling: a mixture of
    ½ cup olive oil, 1 table-
    spoon chopped garlic, and
    salt and pepper to taste
2 whole eggs
1 cup heavy cream

Peel and seed chilies following the directions on page 34. Prepare a smoker using hickory chips. From heavy aluminum foil, fashion a rectangular container with ½-inch sides. Poke holes in bottom and line with parchment so that chilies will not corrode foil. Lay chilies in container and smoke them for 20 minutes, until they have absorbed smoke completely.

Preheat gas grill or barbecue. Toss tree oyster mushrooms in olive oil mixture and grill for 3 minutes, turning constantly. Purée chilies and mushrooms in food processor with eggs. Then, with motor running, slowly add cream.

Grease six 4-ounce ramekins and distribute flan evenly among them. Cover and cook about 12 minutes in a steamer or a water bath, until flan rises and is completely cooked. Unmold and serve warm. (Can be reheated in steamer or water bath.)

ASIAN-STYLE APPETIZERS

Having been raised in the San Franscisco Bay Area with its strong Asian communities and great Asian restaurants, I suppose it was natural that my cooking at Janos would eventually show signs of Asian influence. My interest in Chinese food began when I was ten and my mother decided I was old enough to take the train unescorted to San Francisco. A classmate and I arrived at the depot where my grandfather was waiting. He took us to his office downtown on Montgomery Street and then, while he returned to work, turned us loose to explore the city. The one thing I wanted was fried rice, so we headed for Chinatown. Basking in our freedom from parental supervision, we explored the fish markets, vegetable stands, and food stores. I remember watching entranced as the fishmonger filleted fish after fish to be wrapped in Chinese newspaper and taken home for dinner. I was fascinated by the Peking duck hanging in shop windows and by the unusual displays of vegetables, so different from anything we saw in the suburbs. There was so much to see that it was mid-afternoon before we got our fried rice and tea.

That first sortie into Chinatown set the pattern for shopping in markets wherever I go. The Chinese markets were in some ways no different from the markets in Bordeaux. In both places you find great, fresh local products displayed and sold with passion. The products speak for themselves and have always stimulated my imagination. The three Asian appetizer recipes included here are all fun and interesting twists on dishes commonly found in Chinese menus.

Pork and Shrimp Shao Mai Dumplings   *Serves 4*

One of my chefs, Eric Frisch, was raised in Berkeley, California, and shares with me a love for Asian cooking and a passion for dim sum, those little Chinese breakfast delicacies. He approached me about putting this recipe he developed for shao mai dumplings on the menu. I love it and so do my guests.

You can get shao mai wrappers in Chinese markets.

6 ounces fresh pork butt, cut into cubes

6 ounces medium shrimp, peeled and deveined

4 ounces shiitake mushrooms, medium diced

1 bunch scallions, finely diced

2 poblano chilies, peeled, seeded (see page 34 for directions), and chopped

3 tablespoons chopped ginger

2 tablespoons chopped garlic

1 cup lightly packed cilantro leaves

2 teaspoons chiltepin or red pepper flakes

Salt and freshly ground pepper to taste

16 shao mai wrappers

1 cup Sesame Dipping Sauce (page 68)

Prepare a steamer.

Coarsely grind pork and shrimp together in a food processor and transfer to a large work bowl. Fold in mushrooms, scallions, chilies, ginger, garlic, cilantro leaves, chiltepin, salt, and pepper. Divide mixture evenly among wrappers, placing a spoonful in the center of each. Form dumplings by lifting a wrapper up around the filling and crimping the edges together at the top.

Steam dumplings until they are cooked through, about 8 minutes. Serve with Sesame Dipping Sauce.

Shrimp and Oyster Mushroom Pot Stickers

Serves 4

Shao mai wrappers are available at Chinese specialty stores.

8 ounces shrimp, peeled, deveined, and roughly chopped
4 ounces tree oyster mushrooms, finely chopped
¼ cup finely diced carrot
¼ cup finely diced jícama
1 bunch scallions, finely diced
1 poblano chili, peeled, seeded (see page 34 for directions), and finely diced
3 tablespoons chopped ginger
1 teaspoon chopped garlic
¼ cup chopped lemon verbena (2 teaspoons grated lemon zest may be substituted)
Salt and freshly ground pepper to taste
16 shao mai wrappers
Egg wash made from 1 beaten egg and 2 tablespoons milk
Peanut oil for pan-frying
1 cup Sesame Dipping Sauce (page 68)
4 tablespoons Pickled Ginger (page 120) for garnish

Prepare a steamer.

In a large work bowl combine shrimp, mushrooms, carrot, jícama, scallions, chili, ginger, garlic, lemon verbena, salt, and pepper. Mix well. Lay wrappers out on a work surface and brush edges with egg wash. Put about 1 teaspoonful of shrimp mixture on 1 side of each wrapper. Fold over other side and press edges together to form a good seal.

Steam pot stickers for about 4 minutes. Heat a thin layer of peanut oil in a large sauté pan and fry pot stickers in batches until they are browned, which will take a little less than a minute per side.

Serve 4 pot stickers per helping accompanied by Sesame Dipping Sauce and garnished with Pickled Ginger.

Spring Rolls of Grilled Scallops and Chinese Barbecue Sausage

Serves 4

Chinese barbecue sausage and egg roll wrappers are available in Chinese specialty stores.

6 ounces fresh sea scallops, brushed with olive oil

4 links Chinese barbecue sausage

½ cup fine julienne of carrot

½ cup fine julienne of jícama

¼ cup sliced scallions, cut in ⅓-inch lengths

4 ounces shiitake or tree oyster mushrooms, cut into medium julienne

2 Anaheim chilies, peeled, seeded (see page 34 for directions), and chopped

2 tablespoons chopped garlic

3 tablespoons chopped ginger

3 tablespoons grated lemon zest

1 cup loosely packed fresh mint leaves

Salt and freshly ground pepper to taste

4 sheets Chinese egg roll wrappers

Egg wash made from 1 beaten egg and 2 tablespoons milk

1 cup Sesame Dipping Sauce (page 68)

4 tablespoons Pickled Ginger (page 120) for garnish

4 sprigs mint for garnish

Prepare a gas or wood grill for grilling scallops and sausage and a deep-fat fryer for cooking spring rolls.

Lightly grill scallops for about 1 minute per side and roughly chop them. Grill sausage for about 2 minutes per side and cut them into a medium dice.

In a large bowl, combine scallops, sausage, carrot, jícama, scallions, mushrooms, chilies, garlic, ginger, lemon zest, mint leaves, salt, and pepper. Mix well. Lay an egg roll wrapper on a work surface and brush edges with egg wash. Spread one-fourth of filling lengthwise along wrapper, leaving a ½-inch flap on either side. Roll wrapper around filling, tucking in flaps as you go.

Test temperature of frying oil by sprinkling a drop of water into it. Oil is hot enough if it spits back. Place spring rolls carefully in oil and cook until they are well browned, about 3 minutes. Remove from oil and drain.

Slice each spring roll on the bias into 4 or 5 pieces and serve on a warm appetizer plate. Accompany each with a small cup of Sesame Dipping Sauce and a garnish of Pickled Ginger and fresh mint.

Quail with Grilled Apple Stuffing and Apple Cider Sauce

Serves 4

The rich, butter-grilled apple stuffing goes well with these little birds, keeping them moist and playing against their slightly gamey flavor.

GRILLED APPLE
STUFFING

3 tart apples, peeled, cored, and sliced ½ inch thick
5 tablespoons butter at room temperature
Salt and freshly ground pepper to taste

QUAIL

4 partially boned quail
Clarified butter for sautéing
1 cup Apple Cider Sauce (page 55), warmed with 4 cinnamon sticks (reserve sticks for garnish)

Prepare gas or wood grill. Lightly brush apple slices with some of the butter and grill them until soft, about 2 minutes per side. Let apples cool a bit, then purée with remaining butter. Don't purée too finely; this recipe is best if some small chunks of apple are left. Place stuffing in a medium pastry bag fitted with a large tip.

Preheat oven to 375°.

Stuff quail by piping in apple stuffing. In a large sauté pan, heat enough clarified butter to coat pan, and brown quail on all sides. Transfer to oven and roast for about 10 minutes. Quail is done when breast meat feels firm to the touch.

Divide sauce among 4 large rimmed soup bowls and place a quail in each bowl. Garnish with reserved cinnamon sticks.

*Fish &
Shellfish*

Lobster with Papaya and Champagne Sauce   *Serves 4*

Alain Sanderen, whose restaurant is now drawing rave reviews at the Lucas Carlton in Paris, previously owned L'Archestrate, a restaurant across from the Rodin Museum. Rebecca and I had a memorable lunch there in the spring of 1982. One of the dishes I enjoyed was lobster braised in champagne sauce with cucumber and mint. Even as I was eating I was thinking of how I could adapt the dish to the Southwest. Back in Tucson I began experimenting and arrived at a recipe that is now a mainstay of our seasonal menu and a dish that many consider to be one of our signature items.

It's ironic that this recipe, which so typifies our cuisine, is the only thing I make using a frozen product. The fact is that frozen Australian rock lobster tails work better in this dish than live Maine lobsters because a large lobster tail yields uniform slices that cook up better in a sauce.

The colorful mousse that accompanies the lobster is made by combining Carrot Mousse and Spinach Mousse, both easy recipes in themselves. They can be layered because they have similar densities. Use four-ounce molds.

4 timbales Carrot and Spinach Mousse (use half of recipes on pages 192 and 193)
3 cups dry champagne
2 tablespoons honey
2 tablespoons julienne-cut carrot
1½ cups heavy cream
1½ pounds raw Australian rock lobster tail meat, cut into 1-inch pieces
3 tablespoons chopped fresh mint leaves
1 papaya, peeled, seeded, and cut into 12 slices lengthwise (mango may be substituted in season)

Prepare half of individual recipes for Carrot and Spinach Mousses. Pour into timbales in alternating layers. (I use 2 layers, but you can have more if you like.) Bake as in individual recipes.

In a very large sauté pan, combine champagne, honey, and carrot, bring to a boil, and reduce to ½ cup liquid. This will take about 12 minutes. Add cream and reduce to 1½ cups. Add lobster and simmer until just cooked through, about 4 minutes, adding mint in the last minute of cooking.

Unmold Carrot and Spinach Mousse and center on 4 warm dinner plates. Surround with sauce and lobster meat divided evenly among the plates. Garnish by fanning 3 slices of papaya away from the mousse, with their ends pointing off the edge of the plate.

Baja Bouillabaisse

Serves 4

Eating bouillabaisse in Marseilles was a revelation. In the "bouillabaisse" I'd had in the States, all of the fish and shellfish were cooked together in a thick, very tomatoey broth. In Marseilles, the fish and shellfish were grilled and served separately from the broth. I much prefer the French technique (which is, of course, the original) because it allows each fish to retain its individual flavor. We adapted the French style to our taste using chilies in the saffron-flavored broth and relying on the local cabrilla and shrimp to supplement the scallops, mussels, clams, and stone crab we fly in from around the country. At home, you can use whatever assortment of fish you like as long as it is fresh. As in Marseilles, we serve the bouillabaisse with a rouille (a red pepper and garlic sauce), which can be used to season the broth, dabbed onto the fish, or spread on garlic toast.

ROUILLE

1 large red bell pepper, coarsely chopped
4 tablespoons bread crumbs
2 tablespoons chopped garlic
Salt and freshly ground pepper to taste
3 tablespoons olive oil

To prepare rouille, purée red pepper, bread crumbs, garlic, salt, and pepper in a food processor. Slowly add olive oil to form a thick paste. Set aside.

Preheat grill. Combine all ingredients for broth and bring to a simmer, cooking for about 5 minutes to allow flavors to meld.

CONTINUED ➞

BROTH

4 cups Fish Stock (page 43)
1 large pinch saffron
1 cup dry white wine
2 tablespoons brandy
2 tomatoes, peeled, seeded, and roughly chopped

SEAFOOD

12 littleneck clams, mulched

12 mussels (either black or green lip from New Zealand), mulched

8 large Guaymas shrimp, peeled and deveined

12 large sea scallops, cleaned

4 pieces cabrilla (3 ounces each) or other firm fish of your liking

For grilling: a mixture of ½ cup olive oil, 1 tablespoon chopped garlic, and salt and pepper to taste

4 stone crab claws, cooked and cracked

GARNISH

16 Anaheim chilies, peeled, seeded (see page 34 for directions), and cut into ½- by 4-inch strips

1 zucchini squash, finely diced

1 yellow squash, finely diced

1 red bell pepper, finely diced

8 ounces unshelled English peas (you will need 1 cup shelled)

Garlic toast

Add clams and mussels to broth, cover, and simmer until they open, about 3 minutes. Meanwhile, brush shrimp, scallops, and cabrilla with olive oil mixture and grill. Scallops will take about 1 minute per side, shrimp 2½ minutes per side, and cabrilla 3 to 4 minutes per side depending on thickness.

To assemble, warm chili strips in broth, then place them decoratively in the bottoms of 4 large individual serving bowls. Warm crab claws in broth. Pour ¼ cup broth into each bowl and attractively compose equal portions of seafood in each. Add diced vegetables and peas to remaining broth to cook them slightly, then ladle them with broth into each bowl. With each portion serve a dish of rouille and some garlic toast.

NOTE: Mulch clams and mussels by setting them in a tub of water with ½ cup cornmeal and refrigerating overnight.

Salmon Saffron, Green Lip Mussels, and Sea Scallops

Serves 4

Of the scores of different preparations for salmon in our repertoire, this is one of the most popular. It is a stunning dish with vibrant color contrasts—the yellow saffron sauce forming the backdrop for the pink salmon with its black grill marks, the green lip mussels, and the ivory-white sea scallops. This dish is best served on white or black china, which frames the food nicely.

MUSSELS
- 1 cup dry white wine
- 1 large clove garlic, roughly chopped
- 12 green lip mussels, cleaned and mulched

SAFFRON SAUCE
- ¾ cup dry white wine
- ¾ cup cooking liquid from mussels
- 1 tablespoon chopped garlic
- 1 tablespoon chopped shallots
- ⅓ teaspoon saffron threads
- 1¼ cups heavy cream
- Salt and freshly ground pepper to taste

SALMON AND SCALLOPS
- 4 Norwegian, Scottish, or king salmon fillets (6 ounces each)
- 8 large sea scallops
- For grilling: a mixture of ½ cup olive oil, 1 tablespoon chopped garlic, and salt and pepper to taste

To cook mussels, bring wine and garlic to a boil in a sauce pot and add mussels. Cover pot and cook for 3 to 5 minutes, until mussels have opened completely. Remove mussels and set aside. Strain cooking liquid for use in the sauce.

Prepare gas or wood grill. Put a pot of water on to boil (for reheating mussels later).

To make sauce, combine wine, mussel liquid, garlic, and shallots in a saucepan, bring to a boil, and reduce to about ⅓ cup liquid. Add saffron and cream and reduce to 1 cup. Season with salt and pepper and keep warm while grilling salmon and scallops.

Brush salmon and scallops lightly with olive oil mixture and place on hot part of grill. Form grill marks on salmon by turning fillets 90° after about 1½ minutes, then cook another 1½ minutes on same side before flipping. Cook for another 2 minutes on the second side or until salmon turns translucent and begins to flake. Salmon is best not overcooked.

Form grill marks on scallops also, but cook them for only 2 minutes total.

CONTINUED →

Reheat mussels by immersing them in boiling water for about 30 seconds.

To assemble, divide sauce among 4 plates. Place a salmon fillet in the middle of each plate and surround by alternating scallops and mussels.

NOTE: Mulch mussels by setting them in a tub of water with ½ cup cornmeal and refrigerating overnight.

Grilled King Salmon in Spring Bouquet

Serves 4

GARDEN HERB CREAM SAUCE

2 cups dry white wine
¾ cup Fish Stock (page 43)
1 tablespoon chopped garlic
2 tablespoons chopped shallots
1 cup heavy cream
¼ cup (*total*) chopped tarragon, chervil, cilantro, mint, chive, dill, lemon geranium, lemon verbena, basil (or any combination of these or other fresh herbs you may have)
Kernels from 1 small ear sweet corn
¼ cup peeled, seeded, and chopped tomato

SALMON AND ASPARAGUS TIPS

16 asparagus tips cut at 4 inches
4 long chives for tying bundles
4 king salmon fillets, center cut (6 to 7 ounces each)
For grilling: a mixture of ½ cup olive oil, 1 tablespoon chopped garlic, and salt and pepper to taste
¼ cup American golden caviar for garnish
Nasturtium flowers, pansies, borage blossoms for garnish

Begin sauce by combining wine, stock, garlic, and shallots in a heavy stainless-steel or copper pot. Reduce liquid to ⅓ cup. Add cream and reduce to 1 cup. Mix in herbs, corn, and tomato. Set aside, covered, to keep warm.

Prepare gas or wood grill. Put a pot of water on to boil.

Cook asparagus in boiling salted water until al dente. Remove and immediately plunge into iced water to stop cooking. Keep cooking water hot on stove for reheating asparagus later. Divide asparagus into 4 equal portions and tie them into neat bundles with chives. (If chives are not pliable, dip quickly in warm water.)

Dip each fillet in olive oil mixture and grill quickly on hot grill, 3½ minutes per side. After 1½ minutes on first side, rotate fillets 90° to create grill marks. Continue cooking. Be careful not to overcook.

To assemble, divide sauce evenly among 4 plates. Place grilled salmon on top of sauce. Reheat asparagus by lowering it briefly into reserved hot water, drain, and place one bundle on each salmon fillet. Put 1 tablespoon caviar next to each asparagus bundle, and sprinkle edible blossoms over everything.

Grilled Salmon and Herb Sachet with Sweet Corn and Basil Sauce

Serves 4

For maximum flavor, the salmon in this recipe should be barbecued, preferably over mesquite or hickory wood.

SWEET CORN AND BASIL SAUCE

Kernels from 2 ears sweet corn

1 cup dry white wine

1 tablespoon chopped garlic

1¼ cups heavy cream

2 tablespoons chopped fresh basil

SALMON AND HERBS

½ cup (*total*) finely minced assorted fresh herbs (dill, basil, mint, thyme, oregano, sorrel, fennel, etc., using whatever is available and in proportions to your liking)

½ teaspoon chopped garlic

6 ounces (1½ sticks) butter at room temperature

Salt and freshly ground pepper to taste

4 thick king salmon fillets (6 to 7 ounces each), each cut into 2 thin flat fillets

For grilling: a mixture of ½ cup olive oil, 1 tablespoon chopped garlic, and salt and pepper to taste

4 whole basil leaves for garnish

To make sauce, combine half of the corn kernels, wine, and garlic in a saucepan and bring to a boil. Lower heat and simmer until liquid is reduced to ¼ cup. Add cream and simmer until liquid is reduced to 1 cup. Purée sauce and return to saucepan. (Can be made in advance to this point and refrigerated.) When ready to serve, heat sauce, adding basil and remaining corn.

Prepare barbecue for grilling. Combine herbs with garlic, butter, salt, and pepper, mixing well. Spread butter mixture on skin side of each of 4 fillets. Put remaining fillets, skin side inward, on top of each buttered fillet as if to make a sandwich. Brush each "sandwich" with olive oil mixture. Grill about 4 minutes on each side, rotating the first side 90° after 2 minutes in order to create clear grill marks. Salmon is cooked when its meat is translucent. Do not overcook.

Divide warm sauce among 4 serving plates. Place salmon on sauce, and garnish with whole basil leaves.

Grilled Salmon and Stuffed Morels

Serves 4

This is a perfect dish for spring, when the morel mushrooms are in season and Alaskan king salmon becomes abundant. The richness of Lobster Sauce plays against the earthiness of the morels with their surprise of Scallop Mousse.

SCALLOP MOUSSE

3 ounces sea or bay scallops
2 tablespoons egg white
¼ cup heavy cream
Salt and freshly ground pepper to taste
1 tablespoon finely chopped garlic

SALMON AND MUSHROOMS

16 large fresh morel mushrooms
4 king salmon fillets (6½ ounces each)
For grilling: a mixture of ½ cup olive oil, 1 tablespoon chopped garlic, and salt and pepper to taste

1 cup Lobster Sauce (page 52)

While making mousse, keep all ingredients as cold as possible and work quickly. In a food processor, purée scallops to a smooth paste. With the motor running, add egg white. When white is fully incorporated, add cream and then salt, pepper, and garlic.

Prepare a gas or wood grill for the salmon and a steamer for the morels.

Rinse morels well to dislodge any grit or sand. With a small pastry bag outfitted with a fine tip, pipe Scallop Mousse through the stem into the cavity at the center of the morel. While salmon is grilling, steam morels for about 2 minutes to cook mousse.

Lightly brush salmon with olive oil mixture and place on hot part of grill. Form grill marks on first side by rotating fillets 90° after 1½ minutes. Grill on same side for another 1½ minutes before turning. Then continue cooking for another 2 minutes or until salmon turns translucent and begins to flake. Salmon is best not overcooked.

To assemble, divide Lobster Sauce among 4 warm dinner plates. Place a salmon fillet in the center of each plate. Slice morels in half lengthwise and divide among plates, placing them in a circle around the salmon.

Chilled Salmon with Orange–Green Peppercorn Crème Fraîche and Berry Compote

Serves 4

This striking main course salad combines the succulence of grilled salmon with a tangy compote of berries tossed in balsamic vinegar and sugar. The orange crème fraîche sauce is delightfully refreshing as a base for the dish, its creaminess a natural foil for the hot green peppercorns. A key to preparing this recipe is to grill the salmon 20 minutes before service and let it cool to room temperature. Do not refrigerate the salmon after cooking or it will lose much of its moisture and delicacy.

ORANGE–GREEN PEPPERCORN CRÈME FRAÎCHE
¾ cup crème fraîche
¼ cup fresh orange juice
1 tablespoon green
   peppercorns

BERRY COMPOTE
1 tablespoon sugar
1 tablespoon balsamic
   vinegar
⅓ cup fresh raspberries
⅓ cup fresh strawberries, cut
   in half
⅓ cup orange sections,
   membranes removed

SALMON
4 Norwegian or king salmon
   fillets (6 ounces each)
For grilling: a mixture of
   ½ cup olive oil, 1 tablespoon chopped garlic, and
   salt and pepper to taste

To make sauce, combine crème fraîche and orange juice in a bowl. Stir in peppercorns. Use at room temperature.

To make compote, dissolve sugar in vinegar. Combine berries and orange sections and lightly fold in sugar-vinegar liquid. Use at room temperature.

Prepare gas or wood grill.

Brush salmon with olive oil mixture and grill to medium rare, being sure to make distinct grill marks on first side by rotating fillets 90° after about 1½ minutes. Salmon will cook in 3 to 4 minutes per side. Let cool at room temperature 20 minutes before proceeding.

GARNISH
4 large Belgian endive leaves
12 slices peeled mango
12 strawberries
12 raspberries

To assemble, divide crème fraîche sauce among 4 chilled dinner plates and place a salmon fillet in the center of each plate. Place an endive leaf perpendicular to the fillet, with its tip resting on the rim of the plate. Spoon compote into leaf so that it overflows. Place 3 mango slices on opposite side of salmon from endive leaf, also perpendicular to the fish. Alternate 3 strawberries and 3 raspberries around rim of plate.

Grilled Swordfish with Opal Basil Sauce and Mango Salsa

Serves 4

Grilled swordfish can be at once sweet, succulent, and hearty—if the fish is fresh and of the proper variety. The best swordfish I have found comes from Hawaii, Florida, or around San Diego in California. All of these differ slightly from each other but all are sweet, have a crisp flavor, and are excellent for grilling. In the past few years the market has offered an abundance of swordfish from Taiwan, often called "Pacific swordfish," which is uniformly disappointing and should be avoided.

Swordfish steaks should be cut quite thick so that when they grill, they remain juicy in the center. This recipe pairs a pungent Opal Basil Sauce with a sweet and tangy Mango Salsa. The flavors, inspired by tastes commonly found in Thai cuisine, work perfectly with the swordfish, which is strong enough to assert itself against these tasty condiments.

CONTINUED →

OPAL BASIL SAUCE

½ cup dry white wine

¼ cup Mussel Liquid (page 45) (clam juice or Fish Stock may be substituted)

1 tablespoon chopped garlic

½ tablespoon chopped shallots

1¼ cups heavy cream

3 tablespoons chopped fresh opal basil (other types of fresh basil may be substituted)

Salt and freshly ground pepper to taste

SWORDFISH

4 swordfish steaks (6½ ounces each), cut 1¼ inches thick

For grilling: a mixture of ½ cup olive oil, 1 tablespoon chopped garlic, and salt and pepper to taste

¾ cup Mango Salsa (page 75) for garnish, substituting mint for cilantro

Prepare gas or wood grill.

To make sauce, combine wine, Mussel Liquid, garlic, and shallots in a medium sauce pot, bring to a boil, and reduce to ¼ cup liquid. Add cream and basil and reduce to 1 cup. Season with salt and pepper and keep warm while cooking swordfish.

Lightly brush swordfish with olive oil mixture and place on hot part of grill. Form grill marks on first side by rotating steaks 90° after 1 to 1½ minutes, depending on their thickness. Let them cook another minute or so before turning, then cook on second side for 2 to 3 minutes. Steaks are done when they are firm to the touch, with only a hint of translucence in the center.

To assemble, divide sauce among 4 warm dinner plates and place swordfish in center of each plate. Spoon on salsa so that it cascades off swordfish into the sauce.

Grilled Swordfish with Basil Pesto and Red Pepper Purée

Serves 4

Vaguely inspired by Italian cuisine, this dish really created itself one fall with a simultaneous occurrence of a surplus of basil, an abundance of red bell peppers, and the fall run of swordfish off Catalina Island in southern California. Don't wait for such fortuitous circumstances to make this dish. It's excellent with any great swordfish. A perfect garnish would be tree oyster mushrooms tossed in olive oil, garlic, salt, and pepper and grilled.

RED PEPPER PURÉE

6 red bell peppers, peeled, seeded (see page 34 for directions), and roughly chopped
1 yellow onion, roughly chopped
2 tablespoons chopped garlic
¾ cup Mussel Liquid (page 45) (clam juice or Fish Stock may be substituted)
½ cup dry white wine
Salt and freshly ground pepper to taste
3 tablespoons butter at room temperature

SWORDFISH

4 swordfish steaks (6½ ounces each), cut 1¼ inches thick
1 cup Basil Pesto (page 76)
For grilling: a mixture of ½ cup olive oil, 1 tablespoon chopped garlic, and salt and pepper to taste

To make purée, put peppers, onion, and garlic in a food processor and purée until smooth. Place mixture in a large sauté pan with Mussel Liquid and wine, bring to a boil, and reduce until sauce is thick enough to coat the back of a spoon. Season with salt and pepper, remove from heat, and whisk in butter. Keep warm or reheat before serving.

Prepare gas or wood grill. Cut a deep slit in the longest, thickest side of each swordfish steak to form a deep pocket. Put pesto into a pastry bag and stuff into swordfish pockets. Lightly brush fish with olive oil mixture and place on hot part of grill. Grill to medium rare, making grill marks on first side by rotating fish 90° after 1 or 2 minutes. Cook for 3 minutes on each side. Fish is done when it is firm to the touch, with only a hint of translucence in the center.

Divide Red Pepper Purée among 4 warm dinner plates and place swordfish in the center of each plate.

Grilled Baja Cabrilla with Bay Scallop Salsa   *Serves 4*

Cabrilla is a seven- to forty-pound sea bass fished in the Sea of Cortez. A meaty, clean-tasting fish, it is perfect for grilling and hearty enough to stand up to the hottest of southwestern preparations. Because of its long season—stretching from October until late May—and its origin in the region, cabrilla is popular with both my guests and myself. The salsa provides an excellent contrast of sea and earth elements (bay scallops simmered with sweet corn, black beans, and chilies) that brings out the characteristic texture and flavor of the cabrilla.

4 thick cabrilla fillets
(6½ ounces each)
For grilling: a mixture of
½ cup olive oil, 1 table-
spoon chopped garlic, and
salt and pepper to taste
Salt and freshly ground
pepper
1½ cups warm Bay Scallop
Salsa (page 73)
Chives for garnish

Prepare gas or wood grill.

Lightly brush cabrilla with olive oil mixture and sprinkle with salt and pepper to taste. Grill until medium rare, turning once, about 4 minutes per side. To form grill marks, rotate fillets 90° after 2 minutes on first side, then continue cooking.

Divide salsa among 4 warm dinner plates and serve cabrilla on top of sauce. Crisscross 2 long chives over the top.

Corn Husk–Roasted Cabrilla with Roasted Garlic Sauce

Serves 4

5 large corn husks
1 Anaheim chili, peeled, seeded (see page 34 for directions), and chopped
4 ounces domestic mushrooms, sliced
2 tablespoons butter, cut into small pieces
Salt and freshly ground pepper to taste
4 fillets cabrilla (6 ounces each)
8 medium Guaymas shrimp, peeled and deveined
1 cup Roasted Garlic Sauce (page 52), made with Fish Stock instead of Chicken Stock
2 Haas avocadoes for garnish, cut in half and each half cut into fans

Soak corn husks in water for 1 hour in order to clean and soften them. Remove and shake off water.

Preheat oven to 375°. Toss together chili, mushrooms, butter, salt, and pepper and pat onto surface of cabrilla. Place each cabrilla on a corn husk (reserve fifth husk for use in making ties later) and place 2 shrimp on chili and mushroom mixture. Gather ends of husk together and tie with twine. This will leave a gap down the middle that will allow steam to evaporate. (Cabrilla should not be completely enclosed or it will steam and become tough.) Put cabrilla bundles in oven and roast for about 12 minutes. Fish should be cooked through but still moist and translucent in the center.

To assemble, divide sauce among 4 warm dinner plates. Remove twine and decoratively tie ends of corn husks with strips torn from the reserved husk. Center wrapped cabrilla on sauce and garnish with avocado slices.

Pecan-Breaded Pan-Fried Catfish with Sizzling Chili Butter

Serves 4

2 cups all-purpose flour
1 cup milk
3 eggs
12 ounces shelled pecans, ground
4 ounces Parmesan cheese, grated
Salt and freshly ground pepper to taste
4 catfish (7 ounces each)
Vegetable oil for frying

SIZZLING CHILI BUTTER
6 ounces (1½ sticks) butter at room temperature
1 teaspoon Santa Cruz chili powder
2 teaspoons chopped garlic
2 tablespoons fresh lime juice

1 cup Salsa Fresca (page 71) for garnish

Preheat oven to 375°.

To bread catfish, use 3 shallow containers (pie tins work well). Put flour in the first; milk mixed with eggs in the second; and pecans mixed with Parmesan, salt, and pepper in the third. Coat each piece of catfish with flour, shaking off excess, then submerge it in egg wash, and finally coat it with pecan mixture.

Put ¼ inch of oil in a heavy cast-iron skillet and heat over medium flame. Fry catfish until golden-brown on both sides, about 2 minutes per side. Be careful not to burn breading. Finish in oven, about 7 minutes. Fish is done when it is cooked through but still translucent. Keep warm while making butter.

To make Sizzling Chili Butter, place butter in small, hot skillet and heat until it just begins to brown. With heat still on, quickly add chili powder and garlic, then pour in lime juice. Still working quickly, center catfish on each of 4 warm dinner plates, garnish with Salsa Fresca on top of the fish, and spoon on Sizzling Chili Butter. Serve immediately.

Baja Bouillabaisse

With Levi Rodriguez at his fish shop

*Grilled Baja Cabrilla with Bay
Scallop Salsa*

Grilled Pompano Mimosa

Serves 4

Pompano is a sweet flat fish from Florida with a beautiful silver skin. This pretty presentation brings out the sweet delicacy of the fish. A mimosa is that wonderful brunch drink made from champagne and orange juice.

4 pompano fillets (6 to 7 ounces each), with skin on
For grilling: a mixture of ½ cup olive oil, 1 table-spoon chopped garlic, and salt and pepper to taste
Salt and freshly ground pepper
1 cup warm Mimosa Sauce (page 54)
12 orange sections
¼ cup American golden cav-iar (or if price is no object, substitute any of the fine Russian, Iranian, or Chinese caviars)

Prepare gas or wood grill.

Lightly brush pompano with olive oil mixture and sprinkle with salt and pepper. Grill flesh side down for about 2 minutes. Form grill marks on first side by rotating fillets 90° after 1 minute. Turn pompano and grill for about 1 more minute.

Divide sauce among 4 warm dinner plates and center pompano on sauce. Garnish with orange sections and caviar.

Didier's Hawaiian Red Snapper

Serves 4

For Rebecca's thirtieth birthday Didier prepared a surprise six-course dinner for us at La Réserve that still ranks as our best meal ever. One of the
dishes was fresh rouget (red mullet) fillets steamed on beurre rouge. The
dish was beautiful in its simplicity of design and its blend of simple, perfect flavors. The dappled pink and white skin of the rouget shone ele-
gantly against the deep purple sauce. Hawaiian red snapper, which is
similarly colored and more available to me, works well as a substitute. I
serve the dish as a main course with asparagus and wild mushrooms
rather than as the stark, perfect appetizer Didier prepared for us. The
mushrooms can be grilled, broiled, or sautéed; at the restaurant we use
the grill.

24 cleaned and trimmed
asparagus tips
8 Hawaiian red snapper fillets (3 ounces each), with
skin on
Salt and freshly ground pepper to taste
12 ounces wild mushrooms
(morel, tree oyster, shi-
itake, or any other of your
liking)
For grilling mushrooms: a
mixture of ½ cup olive oil,
1 tablespoon chopped
garlic, and salt and pepper
to taste
1 cup warm Beurre Rouge
for fish (page 59)

Prepare gas or wood grill. As grill heats, lightly
steam asparagus. Remove from steamer and keep warm.
(You can also cook the asparagus in advance and reheat.)

Prepare a steamer for the fish. Lightly salt and pepper snapper fillets and steam for 4 to 5 minutes until fish is
thoroughly, yet lightly, cooked. Center should still be
translucent.

While fish cooks, toss mushrooms in olive oil mixture and grill for about 2 minutes, turning frequently.

Divide Beurre Rouge sauce among 4 warm dinner
plates. On each plate, form a base for your arrangement by
mounding mushrooms beside the rim at any point. Place
two pieces of snapper radiating spoke-like from mushrooms, then compose asparagus spears spoke-like from
mushrooms on either side of snapper fillets.

Grilled Ahi with Stir-Fried Bok Choy and Papaya

Serves 4

Ahi is a sweet, red-fleshed, meaty variety of Hawaiian tuna. When very fresh and cooked medium rare, it has the texture of beef tenderloin. At home I like to use it for fish tacos with black beans, salsa, and flour tortillas. At Janos I sometimes emphasize ahi's Hawaiian origins with this recipe.

MACADAMIA NUT BUTTER

4 ounces salted, roasted macadamia nuts
8 ounces (2 sticks) softened unsalted butter
1 tablespoon fresh lemon juice
Freshly ground pepper to taste

AHI

4 steaks very fresh ahi (7 ounces each), cut at least 1½ inches thick (have butcher remove skin)
For grilling: a mixture of ½ cup olive oil, 1 tablespoon chopped garlic, and salt and pepper to taste

PAPAYA

1 papaya
3 tablespoons fresh lime juice
1 tablespoon honey

Prepare Macadamia Nut Butter, grinding nuts in a food processor. Add remaining ingredients and blend thoroughly. Place butter on a 6- by 8-inch piece of parchment paper along an 8-inch side. Roll into remaining paper to form a log. Freeze. Before using, allow to thaw, but refrigerate or refreeze unused portion.

Preheat gas or wood grill.

Dip ahi into olive oil mixture and grill quickly, turning once. Ahi should be cooked medium rare, 2½ to 3 minutes per side. Any longer and it will tend to be dry. Form grill marks on first side by rotating fish 90° after a minute or so. When done, move to cooler part of grill to keep warm (don't allow fish to cook any further).

Peel and seed papaya. Slice each half into strips ¼ inch thick. Combine lime juice and honey and dip papaya in this mixture. Grill for 30 seconds on each side. Keep warm while stir-frying bok choy.

CONTINUED →

BOK CHOY

2 tablespoons peanut oil
1 head bok choy, roughly chopped
2 tablespoons chopped ginger
Salt and freshly ground pepper to taste
4 tablespoons rice wine vinegar
2 tablespoons sesame oil

To prepare bok choy, heat peanut oil in a very hot sauté pan or wok. Working quickly and constantly flipping ingredients, add bok choy, ginger, salt, pepper, and rice wine vinegar. When bok choy begins to wilt, add sesame oil, flipping ingredients vigorously to combine.

To assemble, divide bok choy among 4 plates. Slice each piece of ahi neatly and fan slices of fish on top of bok choy. Arrange slices of papaya on top of ahi and garnish each portion with 2 slices of Macadamia Nut Butter.

Grilled Ahi with Ginger Cream; Candied Orange and Almond Relish

Serves 4

For a garnish, we add a relish made of candied orange zest, toasted almonds, and raisins. Since it's as tempting as a snack as in a garnish, our recipe makes enough for both.

GINGER CREAM

4 tablespoons chopped ginger
1 tablespoon chopped garlic
1 tablespoon chopped shallots
¼ cup rice wine vinegar
¼ cup dry white wine
¼ cup sake
½ cup Mussel Liquid (page 45) (clam juice or Fish Stock may be substituted)
1 cup heavy cream
Salt and freshly ground pepper to taste

Prepare gas or wood grill.

To make sauce, combine ginger, garlic, shallots, vinegar, wine, sake, and Mussel Liquid in a heavy saucepan. Bring to a boil, reduce heat, and simmer until reduced to ½ cup liquid. Add cream and reduce to 1 cup. Strain and season with salt and pepper. Keep warm.

AHI

4 steaks very fresh ahi
   (6½ ounces each)
4 or 5 Japanese eggplants
   (depending on size),
   unpeeled and sliced
   lengthwise into 16 slices
   ¼ inch thick
For grilling: a mixture of
   ½ cup olive oil, 1 tablespoon chopped garlic, and
   salt and pepper to taste

1 cup Candied Orange and
   Almond Relish (recipe follows) for garnish

Lightly brush fish and eggplant with olive oil mixture. Grill fish until medium rare, 2 to 3 minutes per side, turning pieces 90° after a minute or so on the first side in order to form grill marks. Grill eggplant on hottest part of grill for a total of about 7 minutes. To form grill marks, rotate after 2 minutes on first side, then continue cooking, turning once.

Divide sauce among 4 warm plates. Arrange 4 slices of eggplant on each plate so that they separate the plate into quadrants, with rounded ends toward the rim. Place ahi in the center of eggplant slices and sprinkle with Candied Orange and Almond Relish.

Candied Orange and Almond Relish

Makes 1 pound

3 cups granulated sugar
4 cups water
Zest from 6 oranges, cut into
   strips ¼ inch wide by
   ½ inch long
2 cups whole blanched
   almonds, toasted and
   roughly chopped
1 cup black raisins
Salt to taste

Make a simple syrup by combining 2 cups of the sugar and all of the water. Bring to a boil and add orange zest. Cook to candy zest, about 5 minutes. Remove from syrup, spread on a flat surface, and let dry, then dust with remaining sugar, shaking off any excess. Toss orange zest with almonds and raisins and season lightly with salt. Store in an airtight container.

Fowl

Hickory-Smoked Duck Breast with Raspberries and Peaches

Serves 4

This is a tasty way to serve duck when raspberries and peaches are in season. The smokiness of the breast plays well against the clean flavor of the peaches, while the slightly tart raspberry sauce cuts the richness of the duck. Be sure to start this dish a couple of days in advance in order to give the duck skin time to dry.

4 boneless duck breasts (8 ounces each), trimmed of excess fat and dried in refrigerator for 48 hours
2½ tablespoons packed brown sugar
¼ teaspoon kosher salt
¼ teaspoon red chili powder
¾ cup Peach Purée (page 62), warmed
¾ cup Raspberry Purée (page 62), warmed with 2 tablespoons anisette liqueur and finished with 2 tablespoons butter
1 tablespoon green peppercorns

Trim duck breasts of all excess fat around edges and trim fat cap slightly, leaving a thin layer of fat over each breast. Place breasts fat side up on a rack in refrigerator and allow to dry, uncovered, for 48 hours before use. This helps duck fat to dry so that it renders more easily during smoking. The result will be crisper, less greasy breasts.

Prepare barbecue for smoking.

Make a cure by combining brown sugar, salt, and chili powder; mix thoroughly. Remove duck breasts from refrigerator and rub completely with cure. Let sit for 1 hour. Leave cure on for smoking, since it will caramelize nicely. Smoke duck over hickory until medium rare, about 1 hour over a warm fire, much less if fire is very hot. Divide Peach Purée evenly among 4 serving plates. Slice duck breasts across width and fan on top of puddles of purée. Spoon Raspberry Purée over sliced breasts, sprinkle with green peppercorns, and serve immediately.

Duck Breast with Cranberry-Brandy Sauce; Pears Stuffed with Chestnut Mousse

Serves 4

This recipe needs to be started two days early in order to give the skin of the duck breasts time to dry in the refrigerator.

4 boneless duck breasts *or* 2 whole ducks (4 to 5 pounds each), trimmed of excess fat and dried in refrigerator for 48 hours

CRANBERRY-BRANDY SAUCE

8 ounces fresh or frozen cranberries
1 cup orange juice
3 cups water
1 tablespoon cinnamon
¼ cup brandy
6 ounces (1½ sticks) butter, cut into small pieces

4 Pears Stuffed with Chestnut Mousse (recipe follows)

If you have purchased whole ducklings, remove breasts, reserving remaining meat for another use. Trim excess fat from edges of breasts and trim fat cap slightly, leaving a thin layer. Place fat side up on a rack in refrigerator and allow to dry, uncovered, for 48 hours. This helps duck fat to dry so that it renders more easily during smoking. The result will be crisper, less greasy breasts.

Combine cranberries, orange juice, water, and cinnamon in a pot and cook until cranberries burst. Continue cooking for another 10 minutes. Strain and measure out ½ cup of the liquid into a small saucepan. (Reserve cranberries and remaining juice for another use.) Add brandy and reduce liquid to ¼ cup. Remove from heat and finish sauce by whipping in butter, 1 piece at a time, until fully emulsified. Keep warm while cooking duck breasts.

Preheat oven to 350°.

Heat a sauté pan and sauté duck breasts, fat side down, until well browned. (No oil is needed because breasts will render their own fat.) Turn and cook for 2 more minutes. Place breasts in oven to finish cooking, 5 to 7 minutes. They are done when they feel firm and resilient to the touch. Remove duck from oven and slice thinly across the width. Arrange on individual plates around Pears Stuffed with Chestnut Mousse. Pour sauce over breasts.

CONTINUED →

Pears Stuffed with Chestnut Mousse

Serves 4

10 ounces canned chestnuts
  packed in water
1 egg
1 cup heavy cream
Pinch *each* of cinnamon and
  nutmeg
4 Nellis pears, unpeeled

Preheat oven to 350°. Purée chestnuts in a food processor to form a paste. Add egg and mix thoroughly. While still processing, add cream, cinnamon, and nutmeg. Fit a pastry bag with a medium star tip and spoon in chestnut mixture. Core pears and pipe a rosette of mousse into each, reserving excess for another meal. Mousse can be kept in refrigerator for up to 3 days, but pears should be stuffed just before baking. Place pears in oven and bake for 30 minutes.

Green Tea–Smoked Duck Breast; Spiced Plums

Serves 4

One of my favorite preparations for duck, this Asian-influenced recipe is a departure from our southwestern and French focus. The duck, plums, and stir-fry create a delicious little package of varied tastes when wrapped in a moo shu pancake.

At first glance this dish may appear to be overwhelmingly complex. However, the marinade, cure, and plums can all be made in advance, leaving just a couple of steps for final preparation. Look in Chinese markets for the 10-spice blend and the moo shu pancakes, which are like crêpes but have a more resilient texture. If you can't locate the pancakes, do the dish without them; it will still be splendid.

4 fresh duck breasts
  (8 ounces each), trimmed
  of excess fat and dried in
  refrigerator for 48 hours

Trim duck breasts of all excess fat around edges and trim fat cap slightly, leaving a thin layer of fat over each breast. Place breasts fat side up on a rack in the refrigerator and allow them to dry, uncovered, for 48 hours before use. This helps the duck fat to dry so that it renders more easily during smoking. The result will be crisper, less greasy breasts.

CURE

½ tablespoon Asian 10-spice blend

½ tablespoon Santa Cruz chili powder

½ tablespoon brown sugar

MARINADE

1 tablespoon chopped ginger

1 tablespoon chopped garlic

3 tablespoons granulated sugar

3 tablespoons sesame oil

1 tablespoon soy sauce

1 tablespoon rice wine vinegar

1 tablespoon dry sherry

FOR SMOKING

1 cup loose green tea

½ cup water

4 to 6 charcoal briquets

STIR-FRY

Peanut oil for frying

¼ cup julienne-cut red bell peppers

¼ cup julienne-cut leeks

¼ julienne-cut carrots

¼ teaspoon chopped garlic

½ teaspoon chopped ginger

1 head baby bok choy, sliced

1 teaspoon grated lemon zest

1 tablespoon chopped fresh mint

1 teaspoon rice wine vinegar

4 tablespoons dry sherry

1 tablespoon sesame oil

2 teaspoons honey

Salt and freshly ground pepper to taste

To make cure, put Asian spice blend in a spice grinder and grind it to a coarse powder. (If you don't have a spice grinder, chop up larger pieces and grind mixture to a powder in a blender.) Mix with chili powder and brown sugar. Keep in an airtight container until needed.

To make marinade, combine ginger, garlic, and sugar in a small stainless-steel bowl. Whisk in sesame oil and then remaining ingredients. If made ahead of time, stir well before using.

Four hours before dinner, remove duck breasts from refrigerator and brush liberally all over with marinade. Let sit 1½ hours at room temperature, basting twice. At end of that time, drain breasts and rub liberally with cure. Let cure 1½ hours longer at room temperature.

Prepare barbecue for smoking. Soak the green tea in the water. Using briquets, build a small fire in your smoker. When coals are ashen, spread tea on briquets, reserving some tea to add later. The tea will cause the fire to smoulder and smoke the duck. Place duck breasts fat side down on a grate and smoke until medium rare, about 40 minutes over a warm fire, much less if fire is very hot. Turn ducks skin side up halfway through cooking.

Stir-fry vegetables in a sauté pan or wok coated with peanut oil, starting with red peppers, leeks, carrots, garlic, and ginger. Sauté over high heat until vegetables begin to wilt, about 1 minute. Add bok choy leaves, lemon zest, mint, vinegar, and sherry, sautéing vigorously. When bok choy begins to wilt, add sesame oil, honey, salt, and pepper and cook 45 seconds longer.

CONTINUED →

4 moo shu pancakes
4 Spiced Plums (recipe
   follows)

Heat pancakes over a steamer made by inverting a strainer over a pot of boiling water. Place 1 pancake at a time over the dome created by the upside-down strainer and allow it to heat briefly. Keep pancakes warm by enclosing them in a warm towel while assembling the dish.

Bring all ingredients to temperature so that everything is quite hot for assembly, and have 4 hot dinner plates ready. Remove duck breasts from smoker and slice thinly on a bias across the width. Fan one breast per plate in a semicircle following the rim of the plate. Cut Spiced Plums into quarters. On each plate, arrange 4 quarters in the crescent-shaped hollow at the base of the fanned duck breast slices. Garnish plums with a cinnamon stick. Arrange stir-fried vegetables in a semicircle along a third of the plate's rim, starting next to the duck slices. Fold pancakes into quarters and place one on each plate at the break between the duck and the vegetables, with the point toward the plums in the center.

Spiced Plums

Serves 4

1 teaspoon chiltepin or red
   pepper flakes
1 teaspoon whole cloves
1 tablespoon cracked
   peppercorns
4 Santa Rosa plums, seeded
   and cut into quarters
1 tablespoon thinly sliced
   ginger
4 sticks cinnamon
3/4 cup plum wine
3/4 cup water

Tie chiltepin, cloves, and peppercorns in cheesecloth to make a sachet. Put sachet and all other ingredients in a medium saucepan and simmer covered for 20 minutes or until plums soften. Remove plums from poaching liquid and reduce liquid by half. Pour over plums. Before serving, discard sachet and ginger slices but reserve cinnamon sticks for garnish. If made in advance, reheat to serve.

Roast Free-Range Chicken with Truffled Duxelles and Madeira Sauce

Serves 4

Free-range chickens are raised without hormones or chemicals and are allowed some exercise. The result is a healthier bird that is more flavorful and has a firmer texture than more commercially raised chickens. Unfortunately, these birds often cost three times as much as their pumped-up brethren. This recipe is simple, elegant, and classically inspired. Roasting the chicken whole with vegetables and with a buttery duxelles against its breast produces a succulent, rich dish that is ideal for a small dinner party.

DUXELLES

- 8 ounces domestic mushrooms
- 8 ounces morel mushrooms
- 8 ounces shiitake mushrooms
- 2 ounces truffles, chopped (reserve any juice)
- 3 tablespoons chopped shallots
- 1 tablespoon chopped garlic
- Salt and freshly ground pepper to taste
- 4 cups dry white wine
- 4 ounces (1 stick) butter at room temperature

CHICKEN

- 2 free-range chickens (2½ pounds each), cleaned and with feet and wings removed for stock
- 4 carrots, roughly chopped
- 1 head celery, roughly chopped
- 2 large yellow onions, roughly chopped
- Salt and freshly ground pepper to taste
- 2 heads garlic, unpeeled and cut in half

Set aside 3 whole mushrooms from each type of mushroom—9 in all—to use as garnish later. To make duxelles, coarsely chop rest of mushrooms and put them in a saucepan with truffles, shallots, garlic, salt, pepper, and wine. Bring to a simmer and cook until wine is completely reduced and mushrooms are beginning to dry. This will take about 20 minutes. Toward the end, stir duxelles constantly to prevent scorching. Allow to sit until mixture reaches room temperature. Fold in butter in chunks.

Preheat oven to 450°. With your fingers, loosen skin from chicken breasts. Spread duxelles over breasts, packing it tightly under skin. Mix carrot, celery, onion, salt, and pepper and put some of this stuffing into the cavity of each bird. Put 2 garlic halves into each cavity. Spread remaining vegetables on bottom of a roasting pan. Place chickens on vegetables and sprinkle skin lightly with salt. Roast at 450° for 10 minutes, then lower temperature to 300° and cook for an additional 1 hour and 15 minutes. Chicken is done if juices run clear when flesh is pricked at the thigh. Discard vegetables.

CONTINUED →

2 cups Madeira Sauce (page 55)

Remove roast chickens from oven and let sit for 15 minutes before carving. To make a sauce, simmer reserved whole mushrooms with Madeira Sauce and any truffle juice for 3 minutes; keep warm. Slice breasts and arrange on individual plates along with one disjointed leg and thigh per plate. Pour sauce over breast meat, being sure each plate receives a helping of mushrooms.

Blue Corn and Buttermilk Fried Chicken   *Serves 4 big eaters*

This fried chicken is one of several down-home dishes I put on the menu from time to time. It's always a favorite. At Janos we serve it with Roasted-Garlic Mashed Potatoes, pan gravy, and grilled corn on the cob. The crust is firm, crunchy, and earthy, with a little fire from the chili powder. This chicken is also great the next day for a picnic, or rewarmed with mashed potatoes.

1½ cups blue cornmeal
3½ cups unbleached all-purpose flour
¾ cup Santa Cruz chili powder
1 tablespoon garlic powder
1 tablespoon salt
1 tablespoon freshly ground pepper
2 cups buttermilk
2 free-range chickens (2½ to 3 pounds each), disjointed into thigh, leg, and breast with wing knuckle attached
Vegetable oil or shortening for frying

Combine cornmeal, 1½ cups of the flour, chili powder, garlic powder, salt, and pepper and mix well.

Line up separate containers of the 2 cups remaining flour, buttermilk, and blue corn mixture (in that order). Pie tins work nicely for this. Coat chicken pieces in flour, shaking off excess; submerge them in buttermilk; and then roll them in blue corn mixture, coating each piece well and shaking off excess.

Preheat oven to 375°. Heat 2 inches of oil or shortening in a high-sided iron skillet; it is hot enough when a drop of water makes it spit. Cook chicken pieces in batches, turning so that they brown evenly. As each piece browns, remove it to a rack in the oven so that grease will drain as chicken finishes cooking. Chicken will cook in 15 to 20 minutes depending on the piece. The juice of thigh or leg should run clear when flesh is pricked with a fork.

El Presidio Pan-Fried Chicken

Serves 8 as an appetizer and 4 as a main course

Stumped for a lunch special one day, I came up with this dish, which I thought of as a play on traditional preparations for pan-fried chicken. These croquettes of chicken mousse are given a southwestern twist by the flavoring of chili and cilantro. As we no longer serve lunch, I occasionally offer them as an appetizer at dinner. They also make a great main course accompanied by grilled squash, Black Beans, Salsa Fresca, or Cilantro-Tomato Beurre Blanc sauce.

4 boneless and skinless chicken breasts
3 egg whites
1 Anaheim chili, peeled, seeded (see page 34 for directions), and chopped
1 cup (4 ounces) grated cheddar cheese
2 tomatoes, peeled, seeded, and chopped
4 scallions, finely chopped
1 tablespoon finely chopped garlic
2 sprigs cilantro, chopped
½ cup heavy cream
Salt and freshly ground pepper to taste

BREADING
2 cups all-purpose flour
1 cup milk
4 cups coarse bread crumbs

Vegetable oil or shortening for frying
Sprigs of cilantro for garnish

Cut breasts into chunks and quickly process in a food processor along with egg whites. Do not purée; chicken should be fairly coarse. Fold in chili, cheese, tomatoes, scallions, garlic, chopped cilantro, and cream and season with salt and pepper.

Shape mixture into patties about ½ inch thick. Set out individual containers of flour, milk, and bread crumbs. Dust with flour, dip in milk, and coat with bread crumbs, handling carefully so that croquettes maintain their shape.

Preheat oven to 350°.

Heat ¼ inch oil or shortening in a sauté pan. Add croquettes and fry until golden-brown, turning once. Finish in oven, 7 minutes. Garnish with cilantro and serve immediately.

Roast Poussin and Blue Corn Stuffing; *Blue Corn Muffins*

Serves 4

Poussins are baby chickens. We buy them from a farm in northern California, and at my request the rib cage and breast bones are removed so that the bird is easier to handle when served. This preparation for poussin calls for a blue corn and chorizo stuffing that I first developed in 1980 as a stuffing for Christmas pheasant. In the restaurant, I like using this stuffing with poussin because it makes a hearty and beautiful individual portion. The same stuffing is great with turkey or a larger chicken. As an accompaniment to the poussins you might choose Calabacitas con Queso for a rustic complement or Tree Oyster Mushroom and Chili Sauté for something more sophisticated.

BLUE CORN STUFFING

4 Blue Corn Muffins (recipe follows)
3 brioches (from a bakery)
½ yellow onion, finely diced
2 celery stalks, finely diced
2 hard-boiled eggs, chopped
2 tablespoons chopped garlic
2 teaspoons chopped fresh sage *or* 1 teaspoon dried sage leaves
2 teaspoons paprika
2 tablespoons chopped parsley
Salt and freshly ground pepper to taste
¾ cup Chicken Stock (page 42), warmed
6 ounces chorizo sausage

Prepare stuffing in a large mixing bowl. Break muffins and brioches into medium-size pieces and toss with onion, celery, eggs, garlic, sage, paprika, parsley, salt, and pepper. Ladle warm stock over bread mixture and stir well. Stuffing should be quite moist. Sauté chorizo, breaking it into small pieces, and mix into stuffing. Add more salt and pepper if needed.

POISSINS

4 poussins (1½ pounds each), with rib cage and breast bone removed
Salt and freshly ground pepper to taste
4 tablespoons butter at room temperature
1 tablespoon Santa Cruz chili powder
2 carrots, roughly chopped
2 onions, roughly chopped
3 celery stalks, roughly chopped

1½ cups New Mexico Red Chili Sauce (page 49)

To roast poussins, preheat oven to 350°. Sprinkle poussin cavities with salt and pepper and pack loosely with stuffing. (Put any remaining stuffing into a baking dish to cook separately.) Mix butter and chili powder together to form a paste, and rub skin with this mixture, reserving some for basting. Sprinkle chopped vegetables in the bottom of a roasting pan, and place poussins on top. Roast for 45 minutes, basting twice with butter mixture. Test for doneness by pricking meat at the thigh. Poussins are cooked when the juices run clear. Discard vegetables.

Heat sauce and divide among 4 warm plates. Put one poussin in the center of each plate on top of the sauce and serve immediately.

Blue Corn Muffins

Makes 9 muffins

¾ cup yellow cornmeal
¾ cup blue cornmeal
½ cup all-purpose flour
1 tablespoon baking powder
Salt and freshly ground pepper to taste

1 egg
1 cup milk
Kernels from 1 ear sweet corn
¼ cup finely chopped red onion
1 Anaheim chili, peeled, seeded (see page 34 for directions), and finely chopped
¼ cup finely chopped red bell pepper
½ cup grated cheddar cheese

Preheat oven to 400°.

In a large stainless-steel bowl, combine cornmeals, flour, baking powder, salt, and pepper. In a separate bowl beat egg and milk together and mix in corn, onion, chili, red bell pepper, and cheese. Add this mixture to dry ingredients and mix together. Pour into muffin tins with cupcake liners and bake for 35 to 40 minutes, until a toothpick inserted in the center of the muffin comes out clean.

Quail, Foie Gras, and Lamb Ensemble

Serves 4

I entered this dish in a mystery box cooking competition held in Tucson the first year Janos was open. In a mystery box competition the competitors select from a storeroom of supplies and then have only four hours in which to create and cook a menu for fourteen. This was my first such competition, and since I was among the last competitors, the larder had been severely depleted by the time my turn came. There wasn't enough lamb for everyone or enough quail, so I decided to serve the two together as an entrée. The combination worked so well that I added the foie gras stuffing and put it on my seasonal menu that spring. The judges liked it too and gave me a gold medal.

4 ounces fresh domestic engorged duck livers, with any large veins removed
2 ounces (½ stick) butter
2 ounces cream cheese
4 quail, with rib cage and breast bone removed
Clarified butter for sautéing
Salt and freshly ground pepper to taste
1 pound boneless lamb loin
1½ cups warm Burgundy Sauce (page 47)
1 recipe Pan-Fried Potatoes (page 195)

To make stuffing, purée livers, butter, and cream cheese in a food processor until smooth. Use a pastry bag to stuff quail cavities.

Preheat oven to 400°. In a sauté pan, melt enough clarified butter to coat pan, and sauté stuffed quail until well browned on all sides. Salt and pepper lamb loin and sauté it also, browning it well on all sides. Put quail and lamb in oven and roast for about 12 minutes until medium rare.

Bring sauce and potatoes to temperature at the same time as quail and lamb. Divide sauce evenly among 4 warmed dinner plates. Place 1 quail on each plate with legs pointing to the center and neck to the rim. Slice lamb into 8 noisettes and place 2 on each plate, at either shoulder of the quail. Slice Pan-Fried Potato pie into quarters and place 1 wedge opposite each quail, with the tip pointed toward the quail's legs. Accompany with vegetables of your choice.

Grilled Rabbit with Roasted Pepper Purée and Blue Corn Fritters

Serves 4

Rabbit is included in this chapter on fowl because it tastes rather like chicken and traditionally has been used interchangeably with chicken in many recipes. The addition of Roasted Pepper Purée and Blue Corn Fritters makes grilled rabbit a hearty preparation, perfect for a cold winter day. Although rabbits are available butchered, they are never cut quite the way I like them, so I buy mine whole. To get two servings per rabbit, we remove the front haunches and the rear leg and thigh, extracting the thigh bone to form a pocket for a duxelles stuffing. We also remove the boneless loin from along the back. Each order consists of front haunch, boneless loin, and leg with stuffed thigh attached.

When grilling the rabbit, take care not to overcook the meat. The loin will cook most quickly, followed by the front haunch; the leg and stuffed thigh will take quite a bit longer.

CHILI DUXELLES
- 4 ounces domestic mushrooms
- 2 Anaheim chilies, peeled and seeded (see page 34 for directions)
- 1 ounce shallots, peeled
- ½ teaspoon freshly ground pepper
- 1 cup dry white wine
- Salt to taste

RABBIT
- 2 fresh rabbits (2½ to 3 pounds each), butchered as described above
- For grilling: a mixture of ½ cup olive oil, 1 tablespoon chopped garlic, and salt and pepper to taste

To make duxelles, coarsely grind mushrooms, chilies, and shallots in a food processor. Combine in a medium sauté pan with pepper, wine, and salt. Bring to a boil and reduce until almost all of the wine has evaporated but mixture is still slightly moist. Be careful to stir constantly as the reduction nears completion in order to avoid scorching.

Prepare gas or wood grill. Stuff each rabbit thigh with duxelles, securing openings with skewers or long toothpicks. Brush rabbit pieces with olive oil mixture. Grill rabbit, turning pieces once. As loin and front haunches finish (in about 7 minutes), remove from grill and keep warm. Cook leg and thigh about 7 minutes longer.

CONTINUED →

1 **cup Roasted Pepper Purée**
    (page 61)
1 **large Blue Corn Fritter**
    (8 inches in diameter) (use
    half of recipe on page 124)

Warm Roasted Pepper Purée, and cut Blue Corn Fritter into 8 triangles. To serve, divide purée among 4 warm dinner plates. Slice loins thinly and fan each along the curve of a plate. Slice stuffed thighs and arrange one on the inside curve of each carved loin. Place front haunch to the side of the thigh. On each plate, place 2 fritter triangles point side up in the hollow formed by the carved thigh.

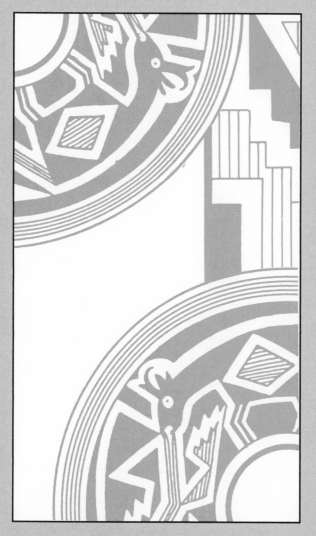

Meat

Veal Pink Peppercorns

Veal Pink Peppercorns served with golden caviar has been a mainstay of our seasonal menu since 1983. I learned to make the sauce from Fred Bramhall, chef at Dudley's in Denver, Colorado. Dudley's was the first nouvelle cuisine restaurant to open in Denver and our favorite restaurant there. One night Rebecca ordered this dish but I ended up eating half of it. The next week I called Fred to volunteer to work in his kitchen when I could get away from my other cooking responsibilities. We added the golden caviar but otherwise the dish is essentially the same one that Fred taught me ten years ago in Denver.

12 pieces boneless veal loin (3 ounces each), pounded thin
¾ cup flour seasoned with salt and pepper
Clarified butter for sautéing

PINK PEPPERCORN SAUCE
1 tablespoon clarified butter
6 ounces domestic mushrooms, sliced
2 tablespoons chopped shallots
1 teaspoon chopped garlic
Salt and freshly ground pepper to taste
⅓ cup brandy
2 tablespoons French dried pink peppercorns
¾ cup dry white wine
1½ cups Veal Stock (page 42)
½ cup heavy cream

4 teaspoons fresh American golden caviar for garnish

Dust pieces of veal in seasoned flour, patting away excess. Coat a large sauté pan with clarified butter and sauté veal in batches. Don't crowd the meat, and constantly scrape the bottom of the pan to remove the particles from sautéing for use in the sauce. Veal cooks in about 1 minute, or 30 seconds per side. Be careful not to overcook. Keep cooked veal on a plate in the warm part of the kitchen.

To make sauce, melt clarified butter in the pan the veal cooked in and sauté mushrooms, shallots, garlic, and reserved scrapings until mushrooms begin to wilt, about 2 minutes. Sprinkle with salt and pepper. Flame by pouring in brandy and igniting with a match. Shake pan until flames die down. Add pink peppercorns and wine and reduce liquid by half. Add stock and reduce to ¾ cup. Add cream and reduce to 1 cup.

To assemble dish, reheat veal in sauce. Divide veal and sauce among 4 warm plates and garnish each with a teaspoon of caviar.

Smoked Veal Loin with
Lobster Sauce and Crayfish

Serves 4

The smokiness of the veal loin is perfectly complemented by the sweet, rich Lobster Sauce, and the crayfish are a spectacular garnish. If crayfish aren't available, large shrimp can be substituted, but they should be grilled rather than steamed. If you do use crayfish, be sure to cook them ahead of time because it takes a while to remove the shell from the tail, but your guests will appreciate the effort. Reheat the crayfish before serving.

1 hickory-smoked veal loin (1½ pounds) (see page 33 for curing and smoking directions)

12 fresh crayfish, steamed and with shells removed from their tails

1 cup warm Lobster Sauce (page 52)

Prepare gas or wood grill for heating veal and a steamer for heating crayfish. Heat veal on grill until hot throughout but not overcooked, from 5 to 7 minutes. Reheat crayfish in steamer.

Carve veal loin into 16 slices. Divide sauce among 4 warm dinner plates and arrange 4 slices of veal inside the rim of each plate so that the slices overlap like a fan. Arrange 3 crayfish with their bodies pointing toward the center of the plate and their heads and antennae pointing away from the veal.

Grilled Veal Chops Marsala and Wild Mushrooms

Serves 4

4 veal chops (10 ounces each), center-cut from veal short loin (have butcher prepare)
For grilling: a mixture of ½ cup olive oil, 1 tablespoon chopped garlic, and salt and pepper to taste
8 ounces assorted fresh shiitake, tree oyster, chanterelle, morel, or other mushrooms
1 cup warm Marsala Sauce (page 55)

Prepare gas or wood grill. Lightly brush veal chops with olive oil mixture and place on hot part of grill for about 4 minutes on each side so that chops are medium rare. Toss mushrooms in olive oil mixture, draining off excess oil, and cook on grill for about 2 minutes, turning frequently.

Place chops in the center of 4 warm dinner plates. Smother each chop with grilled mushrooms, and ladle Marsala Sauce over the top.

Veal Loin Raspberry with Pistachios

Serves 4

In this recipe you can use a basic reduction sauce or you can vary the taste and texture by adding butter or cream.

8 veal loin steaks (3 ounces each)

Salt and freshly ground pepper to taste

Clarified butter for sautéing

2 tablespoons brandy

6 tablespoons raspberry vinegar

3 cups Veal Stock (page 42)

4 ounces shelled pistachio nuts, roughly chopped, for garnish

4 ounces fresh raspberries for garnish

Season veal steaks with salt and pepper. Heat enough butter in a sauté pan to coat bottom of pan, and add steaks. Sauté for about 2 minutes on each side, turning once, until meat is white throughout. Remove from pan and keep warm.

To make a reduction sauce, deglaze pan with brandy and vinegar, reducing liquid by half. Add stock and reduce to 1 cup. This will take 20 to 25 minutes. Pour over sautéed veal and garnish with pistachios and raspberries.

SAUCE VARIATIONS:

• To make a butter sauce, after the second reduction add 4 ounces (1 stick) room-temperature butter cut into small pieces. Remove sauce from heat and whisk in butter, 1 piece at a time. Each piece should be three-fourths emulsified before the next is added.

• To make a cream sauce, add ½ cup heavy cream after the second reduction. Bring sauce back to a boil and reduce to about 1¼ cups.

Roast Prime Rib of Veal
with Armagnac Jus

Serves 6

This roast prime rib makes an elegant and delicious main course for a dinner party or special occasion. It uses a rack of veal, which is comparable to a prime rib of beef only lighter and less fatty. I roast the veal exactly as I would beef, but because it is smaller it doesn't take nearly as long. At the end I like to flavor the cooking juice with Armagnac and accompany the meat with Pan-Fried Potatoes and horseradish. Depending on the season I might also add some asparagus and baby carrots or in winter, turnips and rutabagas glazed with orange and beets simmered in raspberry vinegar and brown sugar.

MARINADE

1½ teaspoons chopped garlic
2 tablespoons Pommeray or other whole-grain mustard
1 tablespoon snipped fresh rosemary *or* ½ teaspoon dried rosemary
Salt and freshly ground pepper to taste
1½ teaspoons soy sauce
1 tablespoon olive oil
1 tablespoon flour

VEAL & ARMAGNAC JUS

1 rack of veal (8 to 10 pounds) (have butcher loosen but keep connected the fat cap and chine bone)
2 carrots, roughly chopped
3 stalks celery, roughly chopped
2 onions, roughly chopped
3 cups Veal Stock (page 42)
3 tablespoons Armagnac liqueur

To prepare marinade, combine garlic, mustard, rosemary, salt, and pepper in a stainless-steel mixing bowl. Work in soy sauce and olive oil and then flour to create a thin paste.

Lift fat cap from veal and liberally rub marinade into meat, covering ends as well. Replace fat cap and prepare veal for roasting.

Preheat oven to 375°. Place carrots, celery, and onions in a large roasting pan. Place veal rack on top of vegetables and roast for approximately 2 hours and 15 minutes or until internal temperature is 115° for medium rare.

To make Armagnac jus, remove veal from roasting pan and allow it to sit while preparing jus. (It will continue to cook slightly.) Pour stock into vegetables, scraping sides and bottom of pan well. Then pour everything into a 2-quart sauce pot. Add Armagnac to sauce pot and simmer gently for 30 minutes. Strain out vegetables, pressing on them to extract their juices, and discard. Degrease jus and correct seasoning with salt and pepper and with more Armagnac if necessary.

HORSERADISH SAUCE
2 tablespoons strong
   horseradish
6 tablespoons sour cream

Combine horseradish and sour cream.

To carve veal rack, use a boning knife to remove fat cap and loosen chine bone. Then carefully remove loin from rib bones. Carve roast into fairly thin slices, figuring 3 per person. Spoon Armagnac jus over sliced meat, and pass horseradish sauce separately. The rib bones can be separated and served alongside the sliced meat, or you can save them for snacking later, after the guests have gone home.

Hickory-Smoked Veal Loin; Roasted Garlic

Serves 4

In the restaurant we serve this veal loin with Black Beans, Roasted Garlic, salsa, and tortillas. The veal must be cured overnight, so start the recipe the day before you intend to serve it.

CURE FOR SMOKING
½ cup packed brown sugar
2 tablespoons kosher salt
2 tablespoons Santa Cruz
   chili powder

Combine all ingredients for cure, mixing thoroughly. (If cure is made in advance, keep it in a well-sealed container.) Rub meat completely and let sit overnight. Leave the cure on for smoking, since it will caramelize nicely.

**VEAL AND
ACCOMPANIMENTS**
1 boneless veal loin
   (1½ pounds) (have butcher
   prepare)
2 cups Black Beans (page
   198)
4 heads Roasted Garlic (recipe follows)
Salsa Fresca (page 71)
Flour tortillas

In a barbecue with tight-fitting lid, start fire with 5 or 6 briquets. While fire is catching, soak 8 ounces of purchased hickory chips in water. When charcoal is ready (about 40 minutes), toss on wet chips which have been strained to remove excess water. Place veal on grill and seal tightly with lid. Smoke until meat is medium rare, about 45 minutes. Remove from grill and slice thinly. Serve with Black Beans, Roasted Garlic, and salsa. Pass warmed tortillas.

CONTINUED →

Roasted Garlic

Roasted Garlic is simple to prepare and goes well with most of the rustic southwestern dishes. We serve it with tacos and with grilled meat, chicken, or fish.

4 heads garlic, intact and
   unpeeled
1 tablespoon olive oil
Salt and freshly ground pepper to taste

Prepare gas or wood grill or preheat oven to 325°. Rub garlic with olive oil and sprinkle with salt and pepper. Place on grill and cook for about 40 minutes, or bake in oven for 1 hour. Garlic is done when it is soft throughout. To serve, slice garlic heads in half around the middle, allowing 2 halves per serving. Your guests can squeeze the cloves from the skin as they like.

Veal Sweetbreads with Pumpkin Purée, Candied Pecans

Serves 4

We cook sweetbreads in two steps, first parboiling and then sautéing them. After parboiling, the sweetbreads can also be grilled or simmered in a sauce. In this recipe the sweetbreads are served on a bright purée of delicately spiced pumpkin. Cilantro Aïoli and Candied Pecans add two other distinctive flavors.

1 lemon, cut in half
1 teaspoon fennel seed
1 teaspoon cracked peppercorns
3 bay leaves
1 teaspoon salt
3 quarts water
2 pounds fresh veal sweetbreads
3 quarts ice water
Flour, salt, and pepper for flouring sweetbreads
2 tablespoons clarified butter
2 to 3 cups Pumpkin Purée (page 61)
½ cup Cilantro Aïoli (page 66)
½ cup Candied Pecans (recipe follows)

Combine lemon, fennel seed, peppercorns, bay leaves, the 1 teaspoon salt, and the 3 quarts water in a pot and bring to a boil. Add sweetbreads, reduce to a simmer, and cook until they are fairly firm to the touch, from 7 to 10 minutes. Sweetbreads will be medium rare at this point; they will finish cooking in the oven. Drain sweetbreads and plunge them into the ice water to stop the cooking process. Pat dry and clean by removing membranes and any veins.

Preheat oven to 375°. Lightly flour sweetbreads in flour seasoned with salt and pepper. Melt butter in a sauté pan. Add sweetbreads and sauté until lightly brown, about 2 minutes per side. Then roast them in oven for 10 minutes to finish cooking.

To assemble, spoon Pumpkin Purée onto the center of 4 warm dinner plates. Place sweetbreads on purée. Using a fine-tipped pastry bag, drizzle Cilantro Aïoli over sweetbreads. Sprinkle with Candied Pecans.

CONTINUED →

Candied Pecans

Makes 1 pound

As with Candied Orange and Almond Relish, we end up munching as many Candied Pecans as we serve. This recipe makes enough that you can snack without feeling guilty.

12 ounces shelled pecans, roughly chopped
4 ounces (1 stick) butter
½ cup Santa Cruz chili powder
1½ cups packed brown sugar

In a large sauté pan, combine all ingredients and cook until butter and sugar caramelize, in 5 to 10 minutes. Remove from heat and pour onto a flat sheet. Mixture will harden as it cools. Break up to serve.

Burgundian Braised Beef Tenderloin

Serves 4

I like to garnish this dish with carved vegetables composed spoke-like around the medallions of beef.

4 center-cut fillets of beef tenderloin (8 ounces each)
Salt and freshly ground pepper to taste
4 cups Veal Stock (page 42)
4 cups burgundy wine

Preheat oven to 375°.

Season fillets with salt and pepper. In an extremely hot dry skillet, brown fillets on all sides. Place beef in an ovenproof dish and pour in burgundy and stock. Braise in preheated oven until medium rare, about 10 minutes.

Remove beef from liquid and cover to keep warm. Pour liquid into a medium sauce pot, bring to a boil, and reduce to 1 cup. This will take about 1 hour.

Strain sauce and divide among 4 warm dinner plates. Place one medallion in the middle of each plate. Garnish with vegetables of your choice.

Medallions of Beef Ginger Port and Red Shallot Butter

Serves 4

Zan Mauler, one of my first sous-chefs, came up with this popular recipe for beef tenderloin. The sweetness of the port is delightfully offset by the ginger in a very rich reduction with veal stock. I like his touch of the Red Shallot Butter, which is served in two cold slices on top of the fillet. The butter can be discarded if the guest so wishes, but it is best when left to melt into the steak. Note that compound butters such as this one can be made in quantity and frozen until needed.

RED SHALLOT BUTTER

2 cups burgundy wine
4 ounces shallots, finely chopped
12 ounces (3 sticks) unsalted butter
Salt and freshly ground pepper to taste

STEAKS

4 center-cut fillets of beef tenderloin (8 ounces each)
1 cup warm Ginger Port Sauce (page 48)

To make butter, combine burgundy and shallots in a small sauté pan, bring to a boil, and reduce until almost dry. Let cool. In a food processor, blend shallots thoroughly with butter. Season with salt and pepper. Cut a sheet of parchment paper in half and mound butter along one long edge of the paper. Roll it into a log. Refrigerate for at least 45 minutes before using, or freeze. If frozen, allow to thaw before cutting, then refrigerate or refreeze unused portion.

Prepare gas or wood grill. Grill steaks to medium rare, about 7 minutes per side, rotating them 90° halfway through cooking first side in order to create grill marks.

Cut 8 slices of ¼ inch each from butter log. Divide sauce among 4 warm dinner plates, place 1 medallion in center of each plate, and garnish with 2 slices of butter placed on top of each steak.

Grilled New York Strips with Beurre Rouge Chili Hollandaise, Slow-Roasted Red Onions

Serves 4

This rich and hearty beef preparation was an immediate hit when we put it on the menu. Slow-Roasted Red Onions add a unifying flavor and an interesting texture. For this dish I like the chewiness and flavor of New York strip steaks although fillets of beef tenderloin work well, too.

4 aged New York strip steaks (10 ounces each), with fat cap trimmed closely
Salt and freshly ground pepper to taste
1 cup warm Beurre Rouge sauce (page 59)
2 Slow-Roasted Red Onions (recipe follows), cut into 8 slices total and warmed on the grill
¾ cup warm Chili Hollandaise sauce (page 65)

Prepare gas or wood grill. Season steaks with salt and pepper and grill to medium rare, about 3½ minutes per side. Divide Beurre Rouge sauce among 4 warm dinner plates and place a steak in the center of each. Top meat with 2 slices of red onion and a strip of Chili Hollandaise sauce.

Slow-Roasted Red Onions

Serves 4

2 red onions, peeled but left whole
2 cups burgundy wine
Salt and freshly ground pepper to taste

Preheat oven to 300°. Place onions in a baking dish and pour in wine. Season with salt and pepper. Roast onions until soft, about 1¼ hours, inverting them after 40 minutes. Slice fairly thickly to serve.

Grilled Pork Chops with Caramelized Onion Sauce

Saguaro cactus

Beef Medallion with
New Mexico Red Chili Sauce

Medallions of Beef with Apple Fritters and Apple Brandy Sauce

Serves 4

This dish is visually very impressive because the fillet sits so tall on the apple fritter. Didier taught me his version at La Réserve. I fell in love with the combination of apple brandy, peppercorns, veal stock, and beef. I decided to add the apple fritter to provide drama to the presentation and to bring out the flavor of the apple brandy. The sweetness of the raisins and brandy is balanced by the sharpness of the cracked black peppercorns studding the fillet.

APPLE BRANDY SAUCE

1 cup golden raisins
½ to ¾ cup port wine, enough to cover raisins
1 tablespoon chopped garlic
1 tablespoon chopped shallots
⅓ cup apple brandy or Calvados
⅓ cup apple cider
1½ cups Veal Stock (page 42)
½ cup heavy cream

MEDALLIONS

4 fillets of center-cut beef tenderloin (8 ounces each)
½ cup cracked black peppercorns

Soak raisins in port for at least 4 hours before using them.

To make sauce, combine garlic and shallots in a medium sauté pan, add brandy, and ignite with a match. Shake pan until flames subside, then add cider and stock, bring to a boil, and reduce to ¾ cup. Add raisins and cream and reduce to 1 cup. Keep warm.

Prepare gas or wood grill.

Rub steaks well with cracked peppercorns and grill over hottest part of grill until medium rare, about 6 minutes per side. Halfway through cooking first side, rotate meat 90° to create grill marks. Move to a cool part of grill to keep warm while preparing fritters.

CONTINUED →

APPLE FRITTERS

4 rounds from a peeled, cored tart apple such as a Granny Smith, cut ½ inch thick

2 to 4 ounces (½ to 1 stick) butter at room temperature, for rubbing on apple rounds

Clarified butter for sautéing

½ recipe Beer Batter (page 90)

Rub apple rounds lightly with room-temperature butter and grill for 1 minute per side to parcook them. Coat a sauté pan with clarified butter; pan should be very hot. Dip each slice of apple in Beer Batter to coat, and sauté immediately before serving.

To assemble, center 1 fritter on each of 4 dinner plates. Place a fillet on top of each fritter. Pour sauce over each fillet.

Chili Duxelles-Stuffed Beef Tenderloin

Serves 4

For this dish, a large fillet is butterflied and stuffed with roasted chili duxelles, trussed with butcher's twine, browned on the grill, and finished in the oven. The tenderloin is then carved into thick slices and served on New Mexico Red Chili Sauce. We toss a confetti of sweet corn and Black Beans on the composed dish for a nice accent of flavor and color.

You will need 3 feet of butcher's twine for tying up the meat.

CHILI DUXELLES

8 ounces domestic mushrooms

3 Anaheim chilies, peeled and seeded (see page 34 for directions)

2 ounces shallots, peeled

1 teaspoon freshly ground pepper

2 cups dry white wine

Salt to taste

Prepare gas or wood grill, and preheat oven to 375°.

To make duxelles, coarsely grind mushrooms, chilies, and shallots in food processor. Combine in a medium sauté pan with pepper, wine, and salt. Bring to a boil and reduce until almost all of the wine has evaporated but mixture is still slightly moist. Be careful to stir constantly as the reduction nears completion in order to avoid scorching.

TENDERLOIN
1 fillet of beef tenderloin
   (2 pounds), center-cut,
   2 inches thick
1 cup New Mexico Red Chili
   Sauce (page 49)
Kernels from 1 ear sweet
   corn, blanched (optional)
½ cup Black Beans (page
   198), rinsed (optional)

Butterfly beef by making an incision down the center of the whole length, cutting almost all the way through. The fillet will open like a book. Lightly pound the two "leaves" to make them slightly wider and thinner.

Mound duxelles along 1 side of length of tenderloin. Fold other side over to encase stuffing. Secure by tying twine around circumference of tenderloin at ½-inch intervals. Brown tenderloin on all sides on grill. Finish cooking by roasting in oven for about 10 minutes; meat should be medium rare. Remove from oven and let sit for 10 minutes before slicing into 8 pieces across the width.

If you are using them, reheat corn and Black Beans in boiling water. Divide chili sauce among 4 warm dinner plates and center meat on top of sauce. Sprinkle each plate with confetti of corn and beans.

Hickory-Smoked Prime Rib of Beef

Serves 14 to 16

This way of preparing prime rib of beef is great for a backyard barbecue. The meat needs no other trappings than creamed horseradish and the potatoes, onions, and carrots that have been wrapped in foil with butter, rosemary, and garlic and cooked on the grill alongside the roast.

1 whole prime rib of beef,
   hickory smoked (see page
   33 for smoking directions)
Enough carrots, onions, and
   potatoes for everyone,
   wrapped all together in foil
   with chopped garlic, fresh
   rosemary, salt, pepper, and
   a few tablespoons butter
Creamed horseradish for
   everyone, made from 1 cup
   strong prepared horseradish and 3 cups sour cream

After prime rib is finished cooking, remove meat from bones and carve enough for your guests. You will have 8 ribs to give to those who want them. Serve vegetables from a bowl, and let guests help themselves to the creamed horseradish, too.

Lamb Noisettes Janos

Serves 4

I created this luxurious preparation for our opening menu and occasionally still put it on our Menu of the Evening. The individual slices of lamb topped with duxelles and gratinéed with Mousseline Sauce are immensely satisfying morsels.

DUXELLES
12 ounces domestic
    mushrooms
6 ounces shallots
1½ cups dry white wine
Salt and freshly ground pep-
    per to taste

LAMB
1 boneless lamb loin
    (1½ pounds)
Salt and freshly ground pep-
    per to taste
Clarified butter for sautéing

1½ cups Mousseline Sauce
    (page 65)

In a food processor fitted with a stainless-steel blade, finely chop mushrooms and shallots. Transfer to a medium saucepan. Add wine, salt, and pepper, bring to a boil, and reduce until liquid has almost evaporated. Set aside.

Preheat oven to 375°. Sprinkle lamb with salt and pepper. Coat a sauté pan with clarified butter and when pan is very hot, sear lamb on all sides. It should be well browned.

Slice lamb into 16 equal slices, or noisettes. Place in one layer on a cookie pan and mound duxelles onto each slice. Cook in oven for 5 minutes, or until meat is medium rare.

Preheat broiler. Top each noisette with Mousseline Sauce and place pan 2 inches under broiler. Broil until Mousseline is nicely browned. Divide noisettes among 4 warm dinner plates and serve.

Roast Loin of Lamb with Pineapple Pear Chutney; Wild Rice Pancakes

Serves 4

2   boneless lamb loins
    (1½ pounds *total*)
Salt and freshly ground pep-
    per to taste
Clarified butter for sautéing
8   Wild Rice Pancakes (recipe
    follows)
1   cup Pineapple Pear Chut-
    ney (page 77)
1   cup warm Ginger Port
    Sauce (page 48)

Preheat oven to 375°.

Sprinkle lamb with salt and pepper. Melt enough clarified butter in a sauté pan to coat pan. Sear lamb on all sides, browning it well. Put in oven and roast until medium rare, about 8 minutes.

Let lamb sit for 5 minutes before carving into very thin slices. Divide slices evenly among 4 warm dinner plates, fanning them uniformly along the inside curve of the rim. Place 2 Wild Rice Pancakes in the hollow formed by the curve of the fan and top the pancakes with Pineapple Pear Chutney. Pour sauce over the meat.

Wild Rice Pancakes

Makes about 15 servings of pancakes

The rice blend I use is fifty percent Texmati rice, thirty percent wild rice, and twenty percent whole wheat kernels. This combination is hearty and crunchy and works perfectly in pancakes or in a rice pilaf.

Clarified butter for sautéing
½   cup chopped yellow
    onion
1   teaspoon chopped garlic
¾   cup rice blend
¾   cup Chicken Stock (page
    42)
¾   cup water
Salt and freshly ground pep-
    per to taste
½   cup finely chopped red
    onion
½   cup finely chopped celery
3   eggs
½   cup flour (approximate
    amount)

Coat a medium sauce pot with clarified butter and sauté yellow onion, garlic, and rice for 2 minutes. Add stock, water, salt, and pepper, cover, and simmer for 20 to 25 minutes or until all liquid is absorbed. Let rice cool to room temperature before proceeding.

In a large mixing bowl, combine cooked rice, red onion, celery, and eggs. Mix in enough flour to create a batter that is thick and sticky enough to form pancakes.

To cook pancakes, heat a nonstick skillet and coat with clarified butter. Using a soup spoon, form cakes 1½ inches in diameter. Fry for about 2 minutes per side or until browned and crisp.

Grilled Pork Chops with Caramelized Onion Sauce; White Beans; Chicken-Apple Sausage

Serves 4

A hearty winter preparation, this dish exemplifies our penchant for giving new twists to time-honored dishes. In this case, we play with the often-served and delicious combination of pork, apples, and onions, known in many countries. Our version calls for grilling thick, center-cut pork chops and serving them on White Beans with an apple-flavored chicken sausage and a sauce of caramelized onions, brandy, and veal stock.

CARAMELIZED ONION SAUCE

Clarified butter for sautéing
1½ cups julienne-cut yellow onions
Salt and freshly ground pepper to taste
¼ cup brandy
1¼ cups Veal Stock (page 42)
½ cup heavy cream

PORK CHOPS

4 center-cut pork chops, cut 2 inches thick
Salt and freshly ground pepper to taste
2 cups cooked White Beans (recipe follows)
8 patties cooked Chicken-Apple Sausage (recipe follows)

Prepare gas or wood grill.

To make sauce, coat a medium sauté pan with clarified butter. Over medium heat, sauté onions with salt and pepper until well browned and sweet, about 20 minutes. Add brandy, ignite with a match, and shake pan until flames subside. Add stock and reduce to ¾ cup liquid. Add cream and reduce to 1 cup. Keep warm.

Sprinkle pork chops with salt and pepper and place on hottest part of grill. Cook for about 12 minutes per side or until pork is medium done.

To assemble, divide White Beans among 4 warm dinner plates and center a grilled pork chop on top of beans. Spoon sauce over each pork chop and garnish with 2 sausage patties per plate.

White Beans

Makes 4 cups

These beans are excellent in a soup. They also freeze well.

6 ounces picked-over white beans, soaked overnight in 3 times their volume of water
1 yellow onion, medium diced
2 bay leaves
3 tablespoons chopped garlic
Salt and freshly ground pepper to taste

Drain and rinse soaked beans. Combine all ingredients in a large sauce pot and add enough water to cover beans by 4 inches. Bring to a boil, reduce heat, and simmer for about 4 hours or until beans are quite tender.

Chicken-Apple Sausage

Makes 8 patties

One August morning during a trip along the northern California coast, Rebecca and I stopped at Cafe Beaujolais in Mendocino for breakfast. The surroundings were warm and homey and our meal was exceptional. I was immediately drawn to the chicken sausage with a hint of apple that was offered as a side dish and began considering its potential for my menu. After some experimentation I came up with this recipe. It is probably quite different from the sausage I ate that morning, but I hope Margaret Fox, the proprietor of Cafe Beaujolais, approves of my version.

6 ounces boneless and skinless chicken breast, roughly chopped
3 ounces (¾ stick) butter at room temperature
1 tablespoon chopped garlic
Salt to taste
¼ cup apple cider
1 medium tart apple such as a Granny Smith, peeled and very finely diced
Clarified butter for frying

In a food processor fitted with a stainless-steel blade, purée chicken breast and butter to a smooth paste. With motor running, add garlic, salt, and apple cider. Transfer mixture to a bowl and fold in diced apple. Refrigerate for 1 hour so that butter solidifies and mixture is easy to handle.

Form sausage into patties 1½ inches in diameter. In a medium sauté pan, heat enough clarified butter to coat pan. Fry patties until well browned on both sides and cooked thoroughly.

Vegetables &
Side Dishes

CARVED VEGETABLES

MANY OF OUR DISHES are served with *tourné*, or carved, vegetables. *Tourner*, or turning, is a French technique for carving vegetables into decorative, seven-sided pieces. The purpose is to create an attractive, uniform shape that makes an elegant presentation. The technique requires a sharp paring knife, or better yet, a special curved paring knife made especially for this process. It also requires many hours of practice on many pounds of vegetables to master. Of all the rudiments of cooking, this is one of the more tedious and difficult because it entails developing a particular dexterity and hand strength that is slightly unnatural. Some of our cooks have suffered weeks of sore hands before they really become accomplished at the task. Once they get it, however, they can turn out hundreds of pieces a night in amazingly little time.

At home, the process doesn't have to be so laborious because you will need relatively few vegetables to serve a dinner party. Choose the vegetables you want to use (zucchini, yellow squash, carrots, potatoes, turnips, and beets work well) and simply cut them into pieces about 1½ inches long and ¾ inch in diameter. Then use a sharp paring knife to carve them into smooth, rounded shapes. Cook the carved vegetables in chicken broth, salted and buttered water, or in the case of beets, orange juice and cinnamon.

GRILLED VEGETABLES

Grilling is an excellent way to cook vegetables for a casual meal or for barbecues. At home during the warm Tucson summers, we regularly cook outdoors, and grilled vegetables such as eggplant, zucchini, summer squash, scallions, and sweet red onions usually make up part of the meal. We use the vegetables whole or cut them into appropriate shapes. For all, the cooking technique is the same: coat the vegetables with olive oil mixed with chopped garlic, salt, and pepper, and grill them over a hot fire until they are cooked through, turning them at least once.

VEGETABLE FLANS AND MOUSSES

Mexican flans are creamy custards traditionally flavored with vanilla and caramelized sugar and served for dessert. The vegetable custards we make are as akin to a savory French mousse as they are to a sweet Mexican flan. They are versatile, making a wonderful first course or an excellent accompaniment to meat or fowl, and they can be made with a variety of ingredients, such as squash, corn, mushrooms, asparagus, leeks, and peppers. In fact, the choice of ingredients is limited only by good taste and imagination. The ingredients should be cooked in ways to bring out their best flavors. For instance, asparagus is fresh and light when simply steamed with lemon, puréed, and strained to remove strings. Acorn squash is wonderful cut in half, seeded, and baked with brown sugar, butter, and cinnamon coating the cavity. The flesh is then scooped out and puréed.

Whatever the vegetable, the ratio of purée to eggs to cream remains about the same: three cups purée to two whole eggs to one cup cream. These amounts yield a little over three cups of mousse. Vegetables with a high water content—for instance spinach, zucchini, and some varieties of mushrooms—should be puréed and strained through cheesecloth before measuring or the mousse will be watery and not set well. Mousses made with denser purées, for instance baked acorn squash, can support slightly more cream to lighten their texture.

Spinach Mousse

*Serves 4 as a first course and
8 as a side dish*

For the prettiest effect, use bright green spinach. We have had the best results from puréeing the raw, cleaned leaves, draining them, and letting them cook in the custard. For this recipe you will need four-ounce or eight-ounce molds, depending on whether you're intending to serve the mousse as a first course or a side dish.

1 to 2 tablespoons butter for greasing molds
12 ounces fresh spinach leaves, washed and stems removed
1 teaspoon chopped garlic
2 large eggs
1 cup heavy cream
Salt and freshly ground pepper to taste

Preheat oven to 375° and butter molds.

Purée spinach leaves and garlic in a food processor until quite smooth. Strain excess liquid from purée by squeezing it through cheesecloth. Return purée to food processor. With motor running, add eggs and, when incorporated, add cream in a steady stream. Season with salt and pepper.

Fill buttered molds and place in a water bath. Cover with foil and bake until firmly set, about 15 minutes for small molds and 25 minutes for large. Remove from oven and allow to sit for a few minutes. To unmold, run a knife around edges and invert.

Carrot Mousse

*Serves 4 as a first course and
8 as a side dish*

**Use four-ounce or eight-ounce molds, depending on whether you're
serving the mousse as a first course or a side dish.**

6 ounces (1½ sticks) butter
12 ounces carrots, cut into
chunks
4 cups Chicken Stock (page
42)
2 large eggs
1 cup heavy cream
Salt and freshly ground pepper to taste

Preheat oven to 375° and use enough of the butter
to grease molds evenly.

In a saucepan, simmer carrots and remaining butter in stock for about 25 minutes or until carrots are quite
soft. Drain carrots, saving buttered stock for cooking
other vegetables or for soup, and purée in a food processor
until completely smooth. With motor running, add eggs
and, when eggs are incorporated, add cream in a steady
stream. Season with salt and pepper.

Fill buttered molds and place in a water bath.
Cover with foil and bake until firmly set, about 15 minutes
for small molds and 25 minutes for large. Remove from
oven and allow to sit for a few minutes. To unmold, run a
knife around edges and invert.

Grilled Eggplant Flan

*Serves 4 as a first course and
8 as a side dish*

This strongly flavored, hearty flan is great with grilled meats or roasts but will overpower more delicate flavors. As a first course, serve it with garlic toast, sliced garden tomatoes drizzled with pesto, and slices of mozzarella. You will need four-ounce or eight-ounce molds depending on whether you are serving the flan as a first course or a side dish.

1 to 2 tablespoons butter for greasing molds
1 medium eggplant, peeled and sliced into ½-inch-thick rounds
For grilling: a mixture of ½ cup olive oil, 1 tablespoon chopped garlic, and salt and pepper to taste
2 large eggs
1 cup heavy cream
Salt and freshly ground pepper to taste

Prepare gas or wood grill, preheat oven to 375°, and butter molds.

Liberally brush eggplant rounds with olive oil mixture and grill until quite soft and completely cooked, about 4 minutes per side. Let cool and purée in a food processor until smooth. With motor running, incorporate eggs, then add cream in a steady stream.

Pour into buttered molds and place in a water bath. Cover with foil and bake until firmly set, about 15 minutes for small molds and 25 minutes for large. Remove from oven and let sit for a few minutes. Unmold by running a knife around edges and inverting.

Roasted-Garlic Mashed Potatoes

Serves 6 to 8

4 heads Roasted Garlic (page 176)
5 russet potatoes, peeled and cut into large cubes
6 tablespoons (¾ stick) butter at room temperature
¼ to ½ cup warm milk
Salt and freshly ground pepper to taste

Squeeze garlic cloves out of skins, place in a food processor, and purée to a smooth paste. Set aside.

Boil potatoes in salted water until soft and completely cooked. Drain. While still hot, transfer them to a mixer fitted with a paddle and mix at medium speed until quite smooth. Add garlic paste and butter and continue to mix, adding enough milk in a stream to make potatoes smooth and a little creamy. Season with salt and pepper and serve immediately.

Pan-Fried Potatoes

Serves 4 to 8 depending on the size of portions

This down-home name describes an elegant dish that in French cooking is called *Pommes Anna*. It is essentially a pie made from layers of potatoes and onion. The whole thing is fried and then cut into wedges to be served. Use a nine-inch nonstick sauté pan for cooking the pie.

Clarified butter for frying
1 large yellow onion, sliced into fine julienne
1 tablespoon chopped garlic
Salt and freshly ground pepper to taste
2 to 3 large russet potatoes (enough to fill pan), peeled
3 tablespoons butter at room temperature

Preheat oven to 350°.

With a little clarified butter, sauté onion with garlic, salt, and pepper until translucent, about 3 minutes. Set aside. Clean pan if there are any cooking bits sticking to it, and coat again with clarified butter.

Working quickly so that they don't brown, slice potatoes into thin (⅛-inch) rounds. Lay enough rounds in concentric, slightly overlapping circles to cover bottom of sauté pan; you should use about one fourth of the potatoes. Sprinkle one third of onion mixture, dot with one third of butter, and season with salt and pepper. Form another layer of potatoes and add onion, butter, salt, and pepper. Repeat 1 more time. Finish with a layer of potatoes.

Place pan over medium heat and sauté for 5 minutes so that bottom layer of potatoes browns. Cover pan with aluminum foil and bake for 30 to 45 minutes, until potatoes are cooked through. They are done when you can insert a knife easily.

Let potatoes cool slightly, then invert onto a large dinner plate to unmold. Cut pie into desired number of servings.

Chayote Potato Gratin

Serves 6

2 whole eggs
1 egg yolk
3 cups heavy cream
2 tablespoons chopped garlic
Salt and freshly ground pepper to taste
Butter or oil for sautéing
1 medium yellow onion, sliced julienne
1 leek, washed and sliced julienne
2 russet potatoes, peeled and thinly sliced
4 ounces Parmesan cheese, grated
1 chayote squash, peeled and thinly sliced

Preheat oven to 375°.

Combine eggs, egg yolk, cream, 1 tablespoon of the garlic, salt, and pepper to make a custard mixture. Set aside.

Coat a sauté pan with butter or oil and sauté onion, leek, and remaining garlic until onion is translucent. Season with salt and pepper.

Coat a small baking pan with butter or oil. Spread a layer of potatoes, cover lightly with custard, sprinkle with onion and leek, and top with Parmesan cheese. Layer chayote over all, and add more custard on top. Repeat until all ingredients are used, ending with a layer of potato and a sprinkling of cheese.

Bake uncovered for 45 minutes, then cover with aluminum foil and bake for an additional 15 minutes.

Zucchini and Chili Latkes

Makes six 3-inch pancakes

One spring, Richard Sax from *Bon Appetit* magazine asked me for some Passover recipes for a feature he was writing. Among the ones I gave him was this variation of latkes, the traditional Jewish potato pancake. My version is wonderful as a side dish with lamb or on its own with sour cream and apple sauce.

1 Anaheim chili, peeled, seeded (see page 34 for directions), and finely chopped
½ cup grated zucchini
1½ cups grated peeled russet potato
½ cup grated peeled jícama
¼ cup grated onion
¼ cup finely chopped cilantro
1 egg, beaten to blend
3 tablespoons matzo meal (all-purpose flour may be substituted)
¼ teaspoon coarse kosher salt, plus more to taste for final seasoning
Freshly ground pepper to taste
Vegetable oil for frying

Preheat oven to 300°.

Combine 3 tablespoons chili (reserve rest for another use), zucchini, potato, jícama, onion, cilantro, eggs, matzo meal, ¼ teaspoon salt, and pepper in a bowl. Mix thoroughly.

Place just enough oil in a large, heavy skillet to coat bottom. Heat over medium heat until hot but not smoking. Carefully add batter to skillet in 3-tablespoon dollops, flattening each into a pancake with a metal spatula. Cook until first side is brown, about 3 minutes. Turn and cook until second side is brown, about 2 minutes. Drain on paper towels and transfer to a cookie sheet. Repeat until batter is used up, adding more oil to skillet as necessary. Keep pancakes in a single layer on cookie sheet.

Place cookie sheet in oven and bake until pancakes are cooked through and crisp, from 12 to 15 minutes. Sprinkle with salt and serve immediately.

Black Beans

Makes 4 cups

I've had varied experiences with the length of time it takes to cook black beans. Even after soaking overnight they can take up to eight hours to soften at high altitudes. In Tucson the cooking time may last up to six hours depending on the season, the minerals in the soil where the beans grew, and the softness of the water. So to avoid any last-minute disappointment, I always cook my beans a day ahead of time.

2 cups dried black beans, soaked overnight in 3 times their volume of water
8 cups (2 quarts) water
Vegetable oil for sautéing
1 yellow onion, medium diced
2 Anaheim chilies, peeled, seeded (see page 34 for directions), and medium diced
3 tablespoons chopped garlic
4 to 8 tablespoons salt
Freshly ground pepper to taste

Pick over and rinse beans, then simmer in unsalted water for about 6 hours if unsoaked and 4 hours if soaked. Add water as needed during cooking to keep beans from burning. Beans should be quite soft and mushy when done but not falling apart.

When beans are within half an hour of being done, heat a little oil in a sauté pan and sauté onion, chilies, and garlic until onion is almost translucent. Add sautéed vegetables, salt, and pepper to beans. Note that quite a bit of salt is needed. Continue cooking until beans are done. Adjust seasoning with more salt and pepper.

Black Bean Cakes

Makes about sixteen 2-inch cakes

Versions of these tasty little pancakes can be found in restaurants specializing in southwestern fare all over the country. Here is my recipe. Black Bean Cakes make a great garnish for beef or veal dishes or a fun and different hors d'oeuvre when topped with sour cream.

1½ cups cooked Black Beans (opposite)
1 tablespoon Santa Cruz chili powder
3 teaspoons cumin powder
½ cup finely chopped red onion
2 whole eggs, beaten
½ cup flour (or enough to bind purée)
Clarified butter for sautéing

Drain beans and purée them with chili powder and cumin. Fold in onion and eggs. Then fold in enough flour to make a sticky, very thick batter.

Put batter into a large pastry bag fitted with a large plain tip. Melt enough butter in a large nonstick sauté pan to coat pan. Pipe batter into pan in 1-tablespoon dollops, which will flatten as they cook to form 2-inch pancakes. Cook for about 2 minutes per side or until cakes brown slightly and are cooked through.

Armagnac and Wild Mushrooms

Makes 12 cups

Armagnac brings out the woodsy flavor of wild mushrooms, which provide a rich vegetable garnish for grilled beef tenderloin or smoked veal loin. Of the three types of fresh mushrooms called for in this recipe, the tree oysters and shiitakes are relatively plentiful year-round and the morels are a tasty addition in the spring when they are in season. But this dish will be excellent with any fresh exotic mushrooms you can find.

Clarified butter for sautéing
2 ounces tree oyster mushrooms
2 ounces shiitake mushrooms
1 ounce morel mushrooms
1 teaspoon chopped garlic
1 teaspoon chopped shallots
Salt and freshly ground pepper to taste
1 tablespoon Armagnac liqueur
2 tablespoons Veal Stock (page 42)
2 tablespoons chopped fresh tarragon *or* 1 teaspoon dried tarragon
2 tablespoons butter at room temperature (optional)

In a medium sauté pan, heat enough butter to coat pan. Sauté mushrooms with garlic, shallots, salt, and pepper until shiitakes begin to wilt, about 1 minute. Add Armagnac and ignite with a match, shaking pan vigorously until flames subside. Add stock and simmer for 2 minutes. Add tarragon. Mushrooms are now ready to serve. Or, for a richer, more luxurious garnish, you can remove mushrooms from heat and whisk in butter.

Tree Oyster Mushroom and Chili Sauté

Serves 4

This tasty sauté makes a quick and easy accompaniment to smoked veal loin, some of the hearty beef preparations, or stuffed poussin. It should be made at the last minute and not overcooked because the mushrooms tend to wilt quickly.

Clarified butter for sautéing
1 Anaheim chili, peeled, seeded (see page 34 for directions), and cut into strips ¼ inch wide and 1½ inches long
1 poblano chili, peeled, seeded, and cut into strips ¼ inch wide by 1½ inches long
6 scallions, cut diagonally in 1½-inch lengths
1 tablespoon chopped garlic
10 ounces tree oyster mushrooms
2 tablespoons brandy
Salt and freshly ground pepper to taste

In a medium sauté pan coated with clarified butter, sauté chilies, scallions, and garlic over high heat for 1 minute. Add mushrooms and brandy and ignite with a match. Shake pan until flames subside, continuing to cook for about 1½ minutes or until mushrooms are lightly cooked but retain their shape. Season with salt and pepper and serve immediately.

Calabacitas con Queso

Serves 6 to 8

Calabacitas is Spanish for "little squash." In this traditional recipe, squash is sautéed with onion; toned with tomato, kernels of corn, and cheddar cheese; and baked in a casserole. At the restaurant we occasionally serve this dish with some of the more traditional Mexican dishes we make. At home it's a perfect vegetable for a casual meal. Use a one-quart, oven-proof casserole for this recipe.

Clarified butter for sautéing
1 large yellow onion, diced small
4 medium zucchini or yellow squash *or* 2 of each, diced medium
2 tablespoons chopped garlic
Kernels from 1 ear sweet corn
3 tomatoes, peeled, seeded, and roughly chopped
2 cups grated cheddar cheese
Salt and freshly ground pepper to taste

Preheat oven to 350°. In a large sauté pan coated with clarified butter, sauté onions, garlic, and squash for about 5 minutes, until fairly soft. Fold in corn, tomatoes, cheese, salt, and pepper and transfer to casserole dish. Cover and bake for 30 minutes.

Desserts

*D*ESSERT OFTEN MAKES THE lasting impression that guests take away from their meal. Our desserts are meant to complement the varied flavors in our cuisine. Like the dinner menus, the dessert selection changes frequently. We lean toward lighter, cooler desserts such as ice creams and fruits but always offer at least one rich, sinful chocolate treat as well. The recipes included here are some of the favorites that our pastry chefs Marianne Banes, Christine Dettloff, and Jill Martin have developed.

Marquise au Chocolat, Crème Anglaise   *Serves 8*

8 ounces semisweet choco-
    late, cut into small pieces
1 cup plus 2 tablespoons
    powdered sugar
6 ounces (1½ sticks) unsalted
    butter, cut into ½-inch pats
5 eggs, separated
¾ cup unsweetened cocoa
    powder
Dash of salt
Dash of cream of tartar
¾ cup heavy cream
Crème Anglaise (recipe
    follows)

Melt chocolate in an ovenproof bowl set over simmering water. Add sugar and mix well. Stir in butter 1 piece at a time, blending well. Remove bowl from over water and add egg yolks 1 at a time, mixing well after each addition. Beat in cocoa. Let cool for 5 minutes, stirring frequently.

Beat egg whites with salt and cream of tartar until stiff peaks form. Gently stir one third of egg whites into chocolate mixture, then fold in remaining whites (do not beat).

Whip cream to soft peaks. Carefully fold whipped cream into chocolate mixture, blending well. Pour into a 9- by 5-inch glass loaf pan (do not use metal). Chill for at least 12 hours.

Just before serving, moisten towel with hot water. Wrap hot towel around pan or mold and invert onto platter. Slice marquise into serving portions and transfer to individual dessert plates. Spoon Crème Anglaise around slices and serve immediately.

Crème Anglaise

Makes 3 cups

7 egg yolks
½ cup sugar
Pinch of salt
2 cups milk
1 piece vanilla bean (1 inch),
   split and scraped

Combine yolks, sugar, and salt in a large bowl and beat until thick and pale lemon colored, 1 to 2 minutes. Scald milk with vanilla bean in nonaluminum saucepan. Remove vanilla bean and set aside. Slowly beat 1 cup of the milk into yolk mixture. Return yolk mixture to remaining milk in saucepan, whisking constantly. Add reserved vanilla bean. Cook over medium heat, stirring constantly, until custard thickens; do not boil. Refrigerate until ready to use.

Nouvelle Gâteau

Makes one 9-inch cake

This cake is rich and airy and almost flourless. Fold in the egg whites carefully because they provide all the leavening. Serve with whipped cream and a garnish of fresh fruit.

6 ounces butter (1½ sticks) at
   room temperature, plus
   butter for greasing pan
5 ounces semisweet
   chocolate
1 cup coffee, reduced to
   3 tablespoons
4½ tablespoons unsifted all-
   purpose flour
¾ cup sugar
Pinch of salt
¼ cup Meyers rum
6 eggs, separated

Preheat oven to 350° and butter cake pan.

Melt butter and chocolate over double boiler. Add coffee and whip well. Remove from heat and gradually whip in flour, sugar, and salt. Whip in rum. Mix in egg yolks.

Beat egg whites until stiff but not dry, and fold into cooled chocolate mixture. Place in a water bath and bake for 1 hour and 10 minutes. Cake is done when a toothpick inserted in the center comes out clean.

Cornmeal Anise Pound Cake;
Spiced Poached Pears

Makes 1 loaf

Butter for greasing pan;
   6 ounces (1½ sticks) plus
   2 tablespoons unsalted but-
   ter at room temperature
1 scant cup sugar
3 eggs at room temperature
6 egg yolks at room
   temperature
1 tablespoon curaçao liqueur
½ teaspoon almond extract
¾ cup plus 1 tablespoon all-
   purpose flour
½ cup plus 1 tablespoon yel-
   low cornmeal
2½ teaspoons baking
   powder
½ teaspoon salt
Zest of 1 orange, grated
2 teaspoons ground anise
Spiced Poached Pears (recipe
   follows)

Preheat oven to 375°. Butter a 5- by 9-inch loaf pan, line it with wax paper, and butter the paper.

In a food processor or mixer, cream butter with sugar until very light and fluffy, about 5 minutes at medium speed. Add eggs and yolks 1 at a time, beating thoroughly, but do not overbeat or mixture will look curdled. Stir in curaçao and almond extract. Sift flour, cornmeal, baking powder, and salt together and fold by hand into egg mixture, smoothing lumps but being careful not to overmix. Fold in orange zest and anise.

Pour batter into pan. Bake until a poker tests clean, 30 to 40 minutes. Cake will turn golden brown and peak in center. It is done when a toothpick inserted in center comes out clean. Cool on a rack and unmold while still slightly warm. Center may sink a little. Serve with Spiced Poached Pears.

Spiced Poached Pears

3 cups port
1 cup water
⅓ cup sugar
⅓ cup packed brown sugar
1 teaspoon coriander
¼ teaspoon crushed black
  peppercorns
¼ teaspoon crushed white
  peppercorns
¼ teaspoon cinnamon
4 whole cloves
Pinch of nutmeg
3 pears, peeled (preferably
  Bosc, Bartlett, or Anjou)

Combine all ingredients except pears in a saucepan and bring to a boil. Reduce heat to low and add pears. To keep pears moist, cover with a circle of parchment paper and simmer until pears are just tender when poked with a toothpick to the core. Remove pears from syrup and cool. Save syrup and when cooled, pour back over pears for storing. To serve, cut pears in half, remove core, and slice lengthwise. Spoon on a little syrup. Serve at room temperature.

Apple Cake

4 cups peeled and chopped
  tart apples such as Granny
  Smith
2 cups sugar
2 cups all-purpose flour
2 teaspoons cinnamon
2 teaspoons baking powder
⅛ teaspoon salt
½ cup raisins
1 cup roughly chopped
  pecans
2 eggs
½ cup vegetable oil
2 teaspoons vanilla
1½ cups Crème Anglaise
  (page 205)
3 tablespoons bourbon

Preheat oven to 350°.

Mix apples and sugar together and let stand for a while. Sift together flour, cinnamon, baking powder, and salt. Combine apples, sifted ingredients, raisins, and pecans. Mix together eggs, oil, and vanilla and add to apple mixture, stirring thoroughly to incorporate all dry ingredients. Batter will be very thick.

Bake until a toothpick inserted in center comes out clean, about 35 minutes. Cool before removing from pan, and serve at room temperature.

Mix Crème Anglaise and bourbon and drizzle over individual pieces of cake.

White Chocolate Cheesecake

Makes one 10-inch cake

2 cups graham cracker
 crumbs
¼ cup sugar
1 teaspoon cinnamon
½ cup melted butter

FILLING
2 pounds cream cheese at
 room temperature
1 cup sugar
6 ounces white chocolate,
 melted and cooled
2 ounces cassis liqueur
4 eggs

SOUR CREAM TOPPING
1½ cups sour cream
⅓ cup sugar
½ teaspoon vanilla

Preheat oven to 350°.

To make a crust, mix crumbs, sugar, cinnamon, and butter together and press into bottom and sides of a springform pan. Bake until lightly browned. Cook while making filling.

Beat cream cheese and sugar together until light and fluffy. Add cooled chocolate and cassis, beating until smooth. Add eggs and beat just until smooth. Pour into crust. Bake 30 to 40 minutes or until set around edges and still slightly soft in middle. Cool slightly.

To make topping, mix together sour cream, sugar, and vanilla and pour over cake. Bake for 5 minutes more. Allow to cool completely before removing from pan, and store in refrigerator. Serve chilled or at room temperature.

Crème Brûlée Tart

Serves 8 to 10

This tart was inspired by the rich French custard called *crème brûlée*, which is topped with a hard crust of caramelized sugar.

1 cup all-purpose flour
2½ tablespoons sugar
Pinch of salt
7 tablespoons chilled unsalted butter, cut into ½-inch pieces
1 egg yolk

CUSTARD CREAM

6 egg yolks at room temperature
6 tablespoons sugar
3 cups whipping cream
1 cup sour cream
1 teaspoon vanilla
4 tablespoons unsalted butter at room temperature, cut into pieces

3 ounces semisweet chocolate, melted
2 cups blackberries
Brown sugar

Make a crust by combining flour, sugar, and salt in a large bowl. Cut in butter until mixture resembles coarse meal. Add yolk and mix until dough just holds together. Flatten into a disk shape and wrap in plastic. Refrigerate for 1 hour (or up to 3 days).

Butter an 8- or 9-inch cake pan. On a lightly floured surface, roll dough out into a circle ⅛ inch thick. Fit into pan, trimming and forming edges. Prick shell, cover with plastic wrap, and freeze until firm (or up to 1 month).

Preheat oven to 400°. Line shell with buttered parchment paper and fill with dried beans or pie weights. Bake 15 minutes. Reduce temperature to 350° and bake 10 minutes longer. Remove paper and weights. Continue baking until brown, about 8 minutes longer.

To make cream, combine yolks and sugar in a bowl and set over a pan of gently simmering water (water should not touch bottom of bowl). Whisk to mix. Add cream, sour cream, and vanilla and continue cooking, whisking occasionally, until very thick, 20 to 35 minutes. Do not boil or custard cream will curdle. Remove bowl from over water and whisk in butter, a piece at a time. Cool for 20 minutes.

Preheat broiler. Spread melted chocolate over crust and cover with berries. Top with custard cream, smoothing surface with spatula. Sift a thin layer of brown sugar over entire top. Broil until sugar caramelizes, watching carefully to prevent burning. Let cool at room temperature, then refrigerate. Serve tart well chilled.

Boysenberry Cookie Tart

Serves 8

½ cup sliced, blanched
  almonds
5 tablespoons sugar
1½ cups (3 sticks) unsalted
  butter
2 tablespoons plus 1½ teaspoons almond paste
1 jumbo egg yolk
1½ cups plus 2 tablespoons
  all-purpose flour

BOYSENBERRY PURÉE
4 cups boysenberries
¾ cup sugar (or more to
  taste)
1 teaspoon fresh lemon juice

Powdered sugar for garnish

Make a cookie crust by grinding almonds with half of sugar in a food processor. Beat ground almonds, remaining sugar, butter, almond paste, and egg yolk in large bowl of electric mixer until light and fluffy. Blend in flour just until mixture forms a ball; do not overmix. Flatten into disk. Wrap dough in plastic or waxed paper and refrigerate while making purée.

Purée berries in a food processor or blender. Transfer to a heavy saucepan and add sugar and lemon juice. Stir over medium heat until thick, about 12 minutes. Strain through a very fine sieve and set aside.

Place a 9-inch flan ring or tart pan with removable bottom on a cookie sheet. Spoon dough into pastry bag fitted with a medium tip and pipe in concentric circles to cover bottom of pan, then pipe around side. (If dough is too sticky to pipe, add a bit more flour.) Leave a little dough for decorating top of the tart. Refrigerate for 30 minutes.

Preheat oven to 375°. Spoon purée into crust. Pipe lattice design over top with remaining dough. Bake until crisp and golden, 45 minutes. Before serving, dust with powdered sugar. Serve at room temperature.

Apricot Tart

Serves 8

TART SHELL

2¾ cups all-purpose flour
½ cup sugar
8 ounces (2 sticks) cold butter, cut into bits
2 egg yolks
¼ cup heavy cream

FILLING

1½ pounds apricots, halved and pitted
2 tablespoons sugar
Apricot glaze (made by heating and straining apricot jam) or strained apricot preserves

Make dough for tart shell by combining flour and sugar. Cut butter into flour mixture until it resembles coarse meal. Mix egg yolks and cream together and pour into flour mixture. Mix with hand until dough forms a ball but is not too sticky. Turn dough out onto a table and "break" it away. (Keeping dough in 1 piece, break off little bits by pushing them away with the palm of your hand.) Continue until entire piece of dough is spread out. Gather dough into a ball and refrigerate for at least 1 hour. On a lightly floured surface, roll dough out to ⅛ inch. Place in a 9-inch tart pan, trimming and shaping edges. Refrigerate until ready to bake.

Preheat oven to 400°. Cut apricots into quarters. Place cut side up in concentric circles in unbaked tart shell. Place as close together as possible. Sprinkle with sugar. Bake until crust is browned and pulls away from pan and apricots are soft, about 40 minutes. Let cool slightly. While cooling, heat apricot glaze, then brush over tart. Serve warm or cold with whipped cream or ice cream.

Orange Pecan Tartlets; Kahlua Caramel Sauce

Makes 6 to 8 tartlets

1 recipe Tart Shell dough
   (page 211)

3 eggs
1 cup packed brown sugar
1 cup dark corn syrup
Rind of 2 oranges, grated
1 tablespoon vanilla
1 teaspoon curaçao liqueur
2 cups pecans
⅓ cup melted butter
Kahlua Caramel Sauce (recipe follows)

Roll out dough to a little more than ⅛ inch and place in tartlet pans. Refrigerate until ready to use.

Preheat oven to 400°.

Beat eggs, sugar, and syrup just to mix. Add orange rind, vanilla, curaçao, and pecans. Add butter and mix well. Pour into tart pans and bake at 400° for 10 minutes, then reduce heat to 300° and bake until set, about another 20 minutes. Let cook completely before removing tartlets from pans. Serve at room temperature on top of Kahlua Caramel Sauce or pass sauce separately.

Kahlua Caramel Sauce

Makes 1½ cups

1 tablespoon butter
1½ cups packed brown sugar
6 tablespoons water
1½ cups heavy cream
2 tablespoons Kahlua
   liqueur

Melt butter in a saucepan. Add sugar and water and stir. Bring to a boil, cover, and cook 3 minutes. Uncover and simmer until soft-ball stage or 238° on a candy thermometer is reached. Remove from heat and let sit for 5 minutes. Add cream and Kahlua and return to stove. Bring to a boil and immediately remove from heat. Serve warm.

Dessert and cognac served in the lounge

Table for two in the Gates Room

The lounge, originally the Stevens' parlor

Mango Ice Cream

Makes 1 quart

2 very ripe mangos, peeled
  and flesh sliced off pit
4 cups (1 quart) heavy cream
9 egg yolks
1 cup sugar
3 tablespoons lime juice
2 tablespoons curaçao

Purée mangos and strain through a medium mesh strain to get rid of strings. Set aside.

Heat cream until scalded. Whisk yolks and sugar together. Put a little hot cream in the yolks to warm them, then whisk in remaining cream, slowly at first and more quickly as yolks approach temperature of cream. Pour back into saucepan and return to stove, cooking until mixture coats back of a spoon. Pour into a bowl set in ice water and cool. Whisk in mango purée, lime juice, and curaçao. Freeze in ice cream freezer following manufacturer's instructions.

Mango Sorbet

Makes 1 quart

These sorbets have a refreshing, not-too-sweet flavor that makes them perfect as a garnish for a chilled soup or as a palate cleanser between courses. For a light dessert, serve them with fruit and cookies.

6 very ripe mangos
¼ cup lime juice

Peel mangos, remove flesh from around pit, and purée completely with lime juice. Strain purée through a medium mesh strainer to remove strings. Pour into an ice cream freezer or sorbet machine and follow manufacturer's instructions.

Strawberry Sorbet

Makes 1 quart

2 pints strawberries, hulled
½ cup sugar (more or less depending on sweetness of berries)

Purée strawberries until they are completely smooth. Add sugar. Pour purée into an ice cream freezer or sorbet machine and follow manufacturer's instructions.

Poached Quinces

Serves 4

1 pound quinces
2 cups sugar
4 cups water
2 vanilla beans, split

Peel, core, and quarter quinces. In a saucepan, dissolve sugar in water, add vanilla beans, and bring to a simmer. Add quinces and poach for 3 hours, adding water and sugar in the same ratio as needed to keep quinces completely covered. Fruit will turn a beautiful rose color and get very tender. Remove from syrup to cool. Then return to cooled syrup and refrigerate. Allow to come to room temperature before serving with ice cream and cookies.

Fresh Fruit Compote

Serves 4 as topping for ice cream

1 cup sugar
1 cup water
1 tablespoon curaçao
1 banana, sliced
2 or 3 strawberries, sliced
6 to 8 raspberries
1 tablespoon butter

Make a simple syrup by combining sugar and water in a saucepan and bringing them to a boil. When sugar is dissolved, remove from heat and add curaçao. If syrup is not to be used immediately, cool and refrigerate. (It will keep indefinitely in refrigerator.)

To prepare fruit, bring syrup to a boil in a skillet over high heat. Remove from heat and add bananas, strawberries, and raspberries; toss to coat with syrup. Return to burner and heat until bubbling. Remove from heat and whisk in butter. Pour over ice cream and serve immediately.

INDEX